MANAGEMENT CASES

Harper's College Press

A department of Harper & Row Publishers

NEW YORK / HAGERSTOWN / SAN FRANCISCO / LONDON

Peter F. Drucker

MANAGEMENT CASES

Library of Congress Catalog Card No.: 77-11758
ISBN:0-06-166403-0

Library of Congress Cataloging in Publication Data

Drucker, Peter Ferdinand, Date—
    Management cases.

    1.   Industrial management—United States—
Case studies.   2.   Management—Case studies.
I.   Title.
HD70.U5D69   658.4′007′22   77-11758
ISBN 0-06-166403-0

TABLE OF CONTENTS

Preface

The fifty cases in this book all deal with specific situations, specific problems, specific decisions—every one of them typical and fairly common in business and other organizations. They are all management situations, management problems, and management decisions—and that means that they deal with what people have to face, what people have to resolve, and what people have to decide. They are thus typical of the kind of situation, problem and decision every one in management commonly faces—the kind of situations, problems, and decisions today's students are likely to face tomorrow. They should thus be approached by students and instructors as cases that ask: How would I handle this?

The cases are organized in eight groups. The first seven follow the organization of my text, *An Introductory View of Management*. They are:

The last group of cases, on Strategy and Structure, focus on the relationship of size to managerial organization and strategy, and on management problems of multinational business and economic integration.

Each case has one primary focus. Each is also—as is every managerial situation, managerial problem, and managerial decision—concerned with both the whole business and the whole person. Each can be read, discussed, and used for one main point and purpose; and each can be read, discussed, and used to gain insight into the complexity of institutions and of human behavior in institutions. Each case can be read and pondered by the student for his or her own learning; each can be discussed either in a "bull session" or in class; each can be used as the topic for a paper. For I hope that the cases are not only instructive but also interesting and entertaining. They deal with real people in real situations.

Peter F. Drucker

BUSINESS
PERFORMANCE

PART ONE

What is
OUR Business?

As long as Bill Callahan could remember he had always worked —indeed lived—in a retail store. His father had owned a small meat market in South Philadelphia—and young Bill had played there as a toddler and gone to work as soon as he was old enough to hold a broom. He had worked in the market weekends while going to school and college; and when he went into the army during the Korean War he found himself almost immediately running a Post Exchange. And Bill loved every minute of it—indeed his idea of heaven was a huge supermarket in which all the cash registers rang all the time.

Bill had known since he was eight or nine that he would own and build a retail chain—and he started the day he was discharged from the army in the mid-1950s. But he also knew that his chain would be quite different from any other. For Bill had deep convictions as to what makes a successful retail business. "No retailer can carry better or even different goods," he argued. "What he can do is first make shopping more enjoyable, more friendly, more fun; and secondly make the retail store a place where people like to work and a place the employees consider their own personal concern." This, according to Bill Callahan, meant three things: First no chain could contain more than a handful of stores—no more than what one owner-manager could manage by example, by frequent visits of inspection, and by personal control. Secondly, each store had to have a center of strength, something that made it distinguished. And finally, the key people in each store—the manager and the departmental managers—had to have a personal stake in the store's success. Callahan's first store was a medium-sized supermarket on the outskirts of a metropolitan community; he got a very cheap rental as the former operator had gone bankrupt. Within three months, Callahan's store was flourishing. "All I did," said Callahan, "was to think through the areas in which a supermarket needs excellence—its meats and produce, for everything else is packged by the manufacturer. So I personally ran the meat and the produce departments, until they were outstanding. Then I thought through how to give distinction to a small store—and I started the first flower and plant department in a supermarket in my area. This completely changed the store's physical appearance and attraction, and the department also makes a good deal of money. Finally I knew why people come back to a store—they like the way they're treated. So I stressed being friendly, being friendly, being friendly, until every employee got the idea." Nine months after the first store opened, Callahan opened the second. He moved over to the new store as manager and gave his successor at the first store a substantial share in the store's profits, with smaller shares for the department managers—all the way down to the women at the check-out counters. Within three years, Callahan had eleven stores in the same metropolitan area.

Then, instead of opening more supermarkets, he decided to start a new chain—a chain of garden centers. He repeated the pattern there—and then shifted to home-service centers for the do-it-yourself home owner, built around hand tools and small power tools. His next venture was a chain of greeting card stores—small, high-turnover, and run by one person. Twenty years after he had started with his first store, Bill Callahan incorporated as "Callahan Associates" with four chains, a total of 40 stores and almost $20 million in sales. Each of the chains had its own general manager who had started out as a checker or clerk and worked his or her way up through store management. Together with Callahan, a financial man, and a personnel man—all former store managers who had started at the bottom—they constituted the company's Executive Committee. The general managers of the chains had a small profit-participation in Callahan Associates and a substantial participation in the profits of their own chain. Each store manager under them had a smaller share in the chain's profits and a substantial share in his store's profits—and so all the way down with every employee with more than eighteen months of service participating in some sort of profit-sharing plan.

Callahan deeply believed that the company had to expand to give people promotional opportunities. And since he also believed that no one chain should grow beyond the point where one man could easily manage it and know every nook and cranny of it, this meant going purposefully into new businesses every four or five years. Accordingly he started in the fall of 1974—almost exactly twenty years after he opened his first store—to look around for the next business to go in. He finally picked two as most promising—a chain of "Outdoor Wear Stores"—blue jeans, boots, Western shirts and so on; and a chain of simple restaurants featuring steak, roast beef, chicken, and so on. However, he knew that he should tackle only one of these at a time—Callahan had learned how difficult it is to get a new venture going and knew that he himself would have to spend most of his time on it for the first two or three years.

It was the policy of Callahan Associates to make all major decisions unanimously in the Executive Committee. In the past that had been very much a formality—the members followed Callahan's lead. But when he brought up the new expansion plans, Callahan ran unexpectedly into serious opposition. Every one agreed that it was time to get a new venture going. Everyone agreed that they had to concentrate on one venture. Indeed everyone seemed to agree that the two areas Callahan had picked offered excellent opportunities. But half the group was bitterly opposed to going into anything that had to do with "fashion" (the Outdoor Wear business), and the other half was as bitterly opposed to going into a "personal service" business (restaurants). "We know a good deal about food and home products," said the first group. "Our customers are housewives and home owners. "Outdoor Wear"—that's kids to begin with; and it is style and promotion and sex appeal—not our bag." "Restaurants," the others argued, "are not for us—we know how to sell *things* to people—but restaurants sell service and atmosphere and have to cook and cater to guests—not our bag."

"All right," said a thoroughly exasperated Callahan, "you have told me what our business is NOT—but how does one go about deciding what it is or should be? You all agree that the market opportunities are good in both areas. So what we need to think through is what it is *we* are, *we* can do, *we* believe in."

How could one go about thinking through these questions?

Case Number 2

What is a Growth Company?

An old-established baker of bread and cakes—distributed widely in one of the country's major metropolitan areas—was bought, during the "conglomerate" craze of the late 1960s, by one of the glamour "go-go" companies of that time. The bakery's stock was selling at 8 times earning on the stock market, the conglomerate had offered 14 times earnings, an irresistable offer. It paid with its own stock that then sold at 37 times earning—so everybody was happy or should have been. The president, a middle-aged but very vigorous member of the founding family—in fact a grandson of the Swedish immigrant who had started the business around 1890—agreed to stay on with a five-year contract.

Six months after the acquisition had been consummated, the bakery's president was called to New York headquarters for a meeting with the president of the conglomerate. "You know, John," the conglomerate president said, "that it is our policy that each of our divisions show 10 percent growth a year and make a return of at least 15 percent pre-tax on investment. Your division is growing only at 1 or 2 percent a year and shows only 7 percent pretax—no more than we can get in a savings-bank account. Our staff people are ready to sit down with you and turn your business around so that it can meet our growth and profit objectives."

"I am afraid," answered the bakery's president, "that they would be wasting their time, and mine. A bakery is not a growth business, and nothing you do can make it into one. People don't eat more bread, or even more cakes, as their incomes go up: they eat less. A bakery has built-in protection against a down-turn; in fact, we'd probably do best in a really serious depression. But our growth isn't going to be faster than that of population. And as for profits, we get paid for being efficient. I know we need to be far more efficient but that would require fairly massive investment in new automated bakeries, and with our price-earnings ratio we have never felt able to raise the kind of money we need. Even if we did automate, our rate of return isn't going to be more than 12 percent pre-tax at best."

"*This is unacceptable,*" snapped the conglomerate's president. "I agree," said the bakery man. "Indeed, this is precisely the reason we gladly accepted your offer to buy us out—we had to free our family's own money for more attractive investments; and all our money was in the bakery. That's also the reason why all of us immediately sold your company's stock. And that's the reason that I am quite willing for you to buy up my employment contract. If you want to run a bread bakery as a "go-go" company, you'd better buy me out—I wouldn't know how to try."

Can one be satisfied with a business that earns less than the minimum cost of capital and cannot raise the capital it needs to become efficient? If not, what (if anything) can be done? And who is right: the man who says that this kind of business cannot be run at a 15 percent profit level, or the man who says that if the market is there, it is management's job to earn a return that can attract the needed capital? Are both wrong? Or could both be right?

Case Number 3

Research Strategy and Business Objectives

Three pharmaceutical companies—*Able, Baker,* and *Charlie*—are among the most successful pharmaceutical businesses in the world. *Able* and *Baker* are very large. *Charlie* is medium sized, but growing fast. All three companies spend about the same percentage of their revenues on research. There the similarity ends. Each of them approaches research quite differently.

Able—the oldest company and the leader in the industry since the end of World War I (also, the most international of the companies)—spends a great deal of research money on one carefully selected area at a time. It picks this area—an exceedingly risky decision—when pure research in the universities first indicates a genuine breakthrough. Then, long before commercial products are available, it hires the very best people in the field (usually those who have made the original breakthroughs in theory) and puts them to work. Its aim is to gain early leadership in a major area, acquire dominance in it, and then maintain this leadership position for years. Outside of these areas, however, the company spends no research money and is perfectly willing not to be a factor at all. (The strategy was originated in the 1920s, when the original work on vitamins was first published. The company hired the Nobel Prize winning chemists who had done the work, brought in the biochemists and pharmacologists and medical people who developed vitamins, and became—within a few years—the world's largest supplier of vitamins. It remains so to this day.) It did not go into another research area, but stayed within the development and exploitation of vitamins until the mid-1930s. Then the sulfa drugs were picked up, again when they were not much more than a "scientific curiosity", and by 1940 the company had acquired world leadership in this field also. To this day it has world leadership in the sulfa drugs which still, despite the rise of antibiotics, supply something like one-third of the market for drugs against infectious disease. The next major move of *Able* did not take place until 1950, when the central-nervous system drugs—the first tranquillizers—

came up. Then the company again went massively into research and emerged with a near-monopoly position in the tranquillizer field. In the mid-1970s, it went heavily into microbiology and cell structure—again, on the basis of very early results in theoretical research. It pays no attention to fields which it decides not to concentrate upon. It totally neglected the antibiotics. It equally neglected, and quite deliberately so, the whole field of fertility control. The company takes big positions in big fields at a very early stage, at great risk, but also—in case of success—at great reward.

The strategy of company *Baker* is completely different. Its research lab, perhaps the most famous in the pharmaceutical industry, works in an enormous number of fields. It does not, however, enter a field until the basic scientific theoretical work has been done. Then it goes to work. The aim is to come up with a small number of drugs in each field that are clearly superior and offer significant advances to medical practice. Of every ten products that come out of its own laboratory, the company itself markets no more than two or three. When it becomes reasonably clear that an effective drug will result from a line of research, the company carefully scrutinizes the product, and indeed, the entire field. First, is the new product likely to be medically so superior as to become the new "standard?" Secondly, is it likely to have major impact throughout the field of health care and medical practice rather than be confined to one specialty area, even a large one? And finally, is it likely to remain the "standard" for a good many years, rather than to be overtaken by competitive products? If the answer to any of these three questions is "No", the company will license or sell the development, rather than convert it into a product of its own. This has been highly profitable in two ways. It has generated licensing income almost equal to the profits the company makes on the drugs it makes and sells under its own name. And it has assured that each of the company's products is considered the "leader" by the medical profession.

Charlie company does no research. All it does is develop. It will not tackle any of the products *Able* or *Baker* companies consider attractive. It looks for areas where a fairly simple, but patentable, development can give it a near-monopoly position in a small but important area. It looks for areas in medical and surgical practice where existing products are not doing a job, and where a fairly simple change can greatly improve the doctors' or surgeons' performance. And it looks for fields that are so small that once there is a truly superior product, there is no incentive for anyone else to go in and compete. Its first product was a simple enzyme—actually known for forty years—to make cataract operations virtually bloodless and greatly ease the eye surgeon's job. All the work that had to be done was to find a way to extend the shelf life of the enzyme. The next product was a very simple ointment to put on the umbilical cord of infants to prevent infection and speed up healing. It has become standard in every maternity hospital throughout the world. The company later brought out a product to replace the toxic solution with which newborn babies used to be washed to prevent infection—again, primarily a matter of compounding rather than discovering. In each area, the world market is so limited—maybe to $20 million—that a single supplier, provided it offers a truly superior product, can occupy a near-monopoly position with a minimum of competition and practically no pressure on price.

The research vice-presidents of all these companies agreed, a few years back, to speak on research and business strategy at a major business school. The chairman of the conference—the Professor of Business Policy at the business school—introduced them at the first meeting. "Dr. A.," he said, pointing to the research director of *Able*, "will talk to us about using science and technology to build a business. Dr. B.—the man from *Baker*—will discuss strategy in a business based on service. And Mr. C.—a research director of *Charlie*—will talk about marketing as the basis of business strategy." What did the chairman mean? And what can one deduce in respect to the business objectives and the basic strategies of each company?

Case Number 4

Success in the Small Multinational

It is commonly believed that multinational corporations have to be very large. Indeed, a fairly popular criterion defines multinationals as companies that have at least two hundred million dollars in sales. But actually, there are a great many small companies that have been outstandingly successful, if only because they are politically so much less visible.

A good example of the small and highly successful multinational company is a small Swiss company, Urania A.G., located in the small town—hardly more than a village—of Glarus in eastern Switzerland. Its history is a very peculiar one; twenty years ago, Urania was on the point of liquidation, totally unsuccessful, and indeed practically bankrupt.

The story actually begins with a man, Christian Bluntschli, now in his early seventies. Bluntschli, who had been educated as an engineer in Zurich, came in the 1920s to Philadelphia's Wharton School as an exchange student. He stayed long enough to get a Master's degree and then a Doctorate. When he went back to Switzerland, he was promptly hired by that country's first business school, the Commercial University in St. Gallen. He became a very successful and popular Professor of Finance and stayed until the late 1950s. Then he went to one of the big Swiss banks as a economist. But he found himself rather bored by the work. When the Wharton School approached him with the suggestion that he come to Philadelphia and join the faculty, he was on the point of accepting.

But before he could resign, the bank's president called him in and said: "I wonder, Bluntschli, whether you would take on a special assignment? We have lent a lot of money to a small company which makes precision gears in Glarus, Urania A.G. We now own about 35 percent of the stock. The company seems to be in terrible trouble; in fact, I strongly suspect that it is completely bankrupt. It seems we should liquidate, but the company is the largest employer in a poor rural area, and we are rather worried about the public relations aspect of letting it go out of business. Could you go down to Glarus and look into the affairs of the company and tell us whether you think that salvage is worth trying?"

When Bluntschli went to Glarus, he found things much worse than anything he had been prepared for. Early in the century, the company had been the world's leading supplier of gears for the then-fashionable cog railways. But cog railways had gone out of fashion, replaced by cable cars and rope tows. And although the

11

company had the right products needed for the manufacture of these replacements, it had never tried to sell them. Instead, it built tremendous service staffs and spare part inventories to service old cog railway customers everywhere. In Japan alone, it had twenty-eight trained people on its payroll to supply spare parts and service to only twelve customers—all of them themselves losing money and going out of business. The people who ran the company had spent all their time and all the company's money on inventing in a wide variety of fields. However, they had never done anything with the patents. Their policy was not to license, but to manufacture. Where they could not manufacture—and in few of the areas in which they had taken out patents did they have any manufacturing capability—they simply did nothing. The more Bluntschli saw, the more depressed he became. But also he was excited by the world-wide service capability the company had built up. Finally—and he himself says, "in a fit of temporary insanity"—he decided that managing Urania was what he wanted to do. He went to his associates in the bank and said: "The company is hopeless. How much do I have to pay you for its ownership?" And before he could recover from his temporary insanity, he owned 100 percent of a bankrupt company with no business, no working capital, and no assets, except for an excellent worldwide service staff.

That was twenty years ago. Today, Urania is one of the most profitable small businesses in the world. It employs only about 900 people. But it is the leader in precision gearing—in specialized transportation such as cable cars, ski tows, mining gondolas, and in the special gearing needed for the equipment to put containers on ships and so on. It actually has manufacturing facilities in about thirty countries, but it only makes one or two parts of each of the patented pieces of equipment it sells. Whatever is standard is contracted out to be made on the spot. It still focuses on service, and especially on design service. But it now charges for service, and makes enough profit on service to cover its entire worldwide payroll. Whatever it gets for selling equipment, minus what it has to pay to its own suppliers, is in effect net profit.

When you ask Bluntschli how he got there, he smiles and says: "I did only the obvious things, the things you find in each textbook." What do you think Bluntschli did that neither his predecessors in the ownership and management of Urania nor his associates in the bank did?

Case Number 5

Health Care as a Business

One of the country's leading industrial manufacturers, a company with a long record of leadership in advanced technology, decided around 1965 that major future growth areas would be in community services, rather than in the traditional "hardware" in which the company has always specialized. One of the fields identified as a major growth area was health care. And so a task force was set up to study the hospital, its management, needs, and direction. The assignment was first to look inside the hospital, not asking the question of what business opportunities it might offer to the company. Only after the task force had decided what the hospital itself should or might be was it expected to concern itself with health care as a business opportunity.

After a year's study, the task force decided that the best way to learn about the hospital was to go into hospital consulting. Accordingly, a small staff was set up to do hospital consulting. It soon became the leading hospital consultant in the country, doing a large number of assignments for all kinds of hospitals—and apparently, doing them well.

At the same time, work was continued on the study and design of the "ideal hospital." In the early 1970s, when the hospital consulting activity had already established itself as highly successful and profitable, the task force people went back to top management and said: "There is no doubt in our minds that the hospital needs major restructuring. In fact, we know what is wrong with the hospital and what it needs. We can design a hospital which will give better patient care more economically. It would be a very different hospital from any that is around now. But we think that within a few years the country will be ready to consider major innovations in the hospital; we are clearly moving toward a severe crisis of confidence in the traditional health care system.

"There are three possible approaches. We can design the hardware for tomorrow's hospital, which will need an incredible amount of advanced technology. This is fully within the competence of this company. It would also be fully in line with the company's tradition. It has always been a manufacturer of advanced equipment for a large variety of industrial and institutional users. It could be the company that has the best and most advanced hospital equipment and at the same time knows what to do with it."

"The second approach is to be hospital designers and hospital builders. We could do what G.E. and Westinghouse are doing in the nuclear reactor field and build—whether for the Government or the Board of a community hospital—a complete hospital that we can then turn over to them to run. And—perhaps even more successfully—we could remodel old and inefficient hospitals—that is, practically all the hospitals in existence today.

"Finally, we could go into the hospital business. Hospital bills are increasingly being paid by "third party interests"—the government, Blue Cross, and insurance carriers. Hospital operating expenses, in other words, are being underwritten. And so are the costs of capital in hospitals. This is, therefore, a possible business opportunity. We could take over hospitals, especially in small and medium-size communities, where the need is great and the hospital usually quite inadequate. We could then build the right hospital and run it at a fairly substantial return on capital—and with a good captive market for our hardware."

In order to understand what each of these approaches implies, what questions does top management have to ask? What kind of considerations apply? What facts, figures, guesses, assumptions need to be tested? What, in other words, would have to be known—or at least discussed—before top management could even address itself to the decision?

Case Number 6

The
Mariner Paper Company

Philip French had come to the Mariner Paper Company of Prairie City, Missouri, during the depression of 1921. Mariner, a very small paper wholesaler in a small hardly industrialized town, was almost wiped out that year—its warehouses were bulging with high-priced low-quality paper bought during the years of the World War I boom with its shortages, and now suddenly practically worthless. Three friends of old man Mariner—the town banker, the town grain storage operator, and a doctor—had bailed him out. The grain storage operator, who knew as little about selling paper as did the other two, remembered that French, who had served under him in the World War I Army and who had impressed him most favorably, had gone to work for a Chicago paper merchant as a salesman and had made it to district manager. Accordingly, French was made general manager of Mariner.

French proved himself as able a manager and businessman as he had been a salesman. He built Mariner into the leading independent merchant chain in the Midwest. He stayed out of the big cities with their tough competition and their well-financed large houses. But he added a small paper merchant here and there—in Sioux City and in Madison, Wisconsin; in Denver and in San Antonio, and so on. By 1950, Mariner had 29 houses doing an annual business of well over $60 million and netting a respectable 5% of sales—high for a paper merchant. French had tailored each house to the business of its area. Some were purely paper merchants. Others, in smaller places, carried other supplies for the printer, especially inks. In still smaller places, they added office equipment and school supplies. As a result, each house had enough business to carry its management and overhead—and to be able to offer attractive rewards to a bright, hard-working and aggressive (and well paid) sales manager. However, French kept all major decisions in his hand.

Mariner grew rapidly—until the mid-1950s. Two things happened then, simultaneously. French, who had always been as strong as an ox, suddenly aged. Barely 60, he seemed much older—when only a few years ago he had seemed a young man not yet out of his twenties. And the paper business got rough—lots of competition, lots of price cutting, lots of new ideas upsetting old applecarts. One big paper company (West Virginia) began to sell direct instead of through merchants; another one (Champion) bought up merchants and built its own national chain, and so on.

French owned only a small block of Mariner stock. But the main owners, the heirs of the three men who had put him in in the first place, rarely interfered. They had their own work—one as a doctor in Chicago, one as a businessman in Minneapolis, one as head of an advertising agency in St. Louis. They stayed, however, very close to the business, met each month for a two-day Board meeting and kept each other informed. Having grown up together, they also remained close friends.

After a board meeting, the doctor did not hesitate to call up the other two and to propose a private meeting in Chicago. At the meeting, he began, "I am worried about French. He has all the signs of a fairly advanced and rapidly deteriorating kind of atherosclerosis: the blue, mottled skin tone; the sudden lapses of attention; the trembling hands. I don't think he ought to carry the load much longer, and I am afraid he won't be able to in any event. We owe it to him to think about his successor and the future of Mariner. We owe it to the 680 employees. We owe it to ourselves and our families—and to French, the only other major stockholder as well. I don't want to be an alarmist, but I have seen enough people who look like him. One day he'll keel over with a coronary or a cerebral hemorrhage—even if we relieve him, I am afraid. And we better be prepared—if we wait until it happens, it will be too late."

The other two both agreed. They too had seen the deterioration in French. All three, it seemed, had also given serious thought to the question of what should be done with their company. But the three found themselves in total disagreement.

One of the three said, "It's obvious we'd better sell Mariner to one of the big paper companies, and do it soon. There is no place in this economy for the independent paper merchant anymore. The biggest ones—Crown Zellerbach or Champion—have their own merchant chains. Others, such as West Virginia, do without the merchant. With today's means of communication and transportation, he does not fulfill a function; he just adds costs. If we don't sell soon, before the paper manufacturers discover that they don't need the merchant, we'll just wither on the vine. And anyhow, if we wait much longer, the Anti-Trust Division is going to put a stop to such a sale. So let's move fast—let's hit International Paper or St. Regis or one of the other big companies right away."

"I just don't understand you," the next man said. "Maybe things are going to be rough for the big paper merchant in the big cities. But there'll always be a lot of small printers who need a merchant and whom a manufacturer cannot reach. And a merchant chain captive to a manufacturer cannot sell. For these printers need much more variety of paper than any manufacturer, even the biggest one, can supply. But Mariner has to become a printer's supplier, not just a paper merchant. Paper is at most one third of what the printer buys—yet to sell paper we have to know all about the printer's business and his technology, have to know more about it than the printer does. We make the most money in the smaller houses that handle printing supplies. This is our opportunity; inks, presses, felts, chemicals. We could triple our volume and our profits without adding on one single salesman."

"You are both talking of yesterday's business, fellows," said the third man. "The big paper market and the big market for what we still call 'printers' supplies' are the big companies. Look at the growth of office reproduction—that's where the market is. Our salesmen still try to peddle magazine papers, yet the big growth market is in computer tapes and punch cards, papers for office reproduction, duplicating machines, and inks, and so on—all products our manufacturers don't make and we don't sell. One good industrial customer is worth five small commercial printers—and no one gives him service today. We may have to buy this or that specialty company—maybe one for making duplicator papers, maybe one for inks. Or we might get the stuff in Europe—though I think there are enough manufacturers in this country eager for distribution systems such as we could build. And no one has yet beaten us to it, whereas there are hundreds of salesmen out to sell the printers and dozens of paper company representatives selling direct without benefit of merchant."

You are not expected to know anything about this industry—or to find out anything about it. Assume all three men know what the facts are—and are right about them. How does one test which of these three different approaches to the question "What should our business be?" is serious and worth careful study? What would Mariner Paper Company have to have to be able to pursue each of these three lines? Can one eliminate any of these approaches as inappropriate, not feasible and not worth serious consideration?

Case Number 7

The Downtown Department Store

Before the great East Texas oil boom of the 1920s, the town of Twin Forks, Texas, barely deserved to be called a "cow town." And its biggest establishment, the DOWNTOWN DEPARTMENT STORE, despite its grandiose name, was hardly more than a crossroads general store. With the oil boom, however, Twin Forks came to life— and so did DOWNTOWN DEPARTMENT STORE. The town kept right on growing, especially as its local oil was found to be so rich in petrochemicals that one big chemical company after the other moved in. The growth continued right on through the 1930s, took another big leap forward during the years of World War II—and then really started going in earnest.

DOWNTOWN grew even faster than the town. Young Frank Bohannon, the son of the store's founder, had been ready to leave the town in disgust and look for a livelier place when the boom hit. Instead, he became the town's leading booster—and unlike a good many others, he believed his own forecasts and managed his store according to them. In 1934, when the rest of the nation seemed ready to return the country to the Indians, Frank built the biggest department store anybody in the region had ever heard of or dreamt of—and the new "downtown" center of Twin Forks promptly followed him. It was Bohannon who introduced fashion goods into Twin Forks (people formerly had to go at least as far as Dallas for them). It was Bohannon who started credit selling, charge accounts, an interior decorator, and full-page four-color advertisements in the Sunday papers.

In 1959, the store sold almost $50 million—and net profit ran at a rate of 9%, or $4,500,000 a year. in 1959, Frank Bohannon also died. All his money, it was found, was in DOWNTOWN stock, of which he owned 97½%. The stock was unlisted, of course. And so with a heavy heart the heirs, hardpressed for cash to pay estate taxes, sold a 51% interest in the store to Midwest Department Stores, one of the country's leading department store chains. However, it was agreed that Frank Bohannon's younger brother, Fred—who had been General Manager under his brother for many years—would stay on as President and General Manager until death or retirement.

1959 was the best year the store was to see. The dollar value of sales did not go down, but actual volume remained pretty much the same. And profits went down, inexorably. For a short time the efficiencies in purchasing, inventory control, personnel management and accounting which Midwest's well-trained staff people could introduce into what had been an enthusiastic but somewhat slipshod operation, concealed this. But from 1966 on, actual profits showed decline year after year. It was not hard to find reasons. Sears had opened a big full-time department store with a huge parking lot at the outskirts of the town. The downtown area was deteriorating. Neiman-Marcus from Dallas actively wooed the wealthy customers, offering them a free airplane trip to Dallas and, with purchases over $250, a free stay at a Dallas luxury hotel overnight. The poorer customers in turn were apparently lured away by the discount houses. And so one valid reason for doing badly appeared after the other.

What to do about it was not so easy or obvious. DOWNTOWN made half-hearted attempts and opened two suburban shopping centers. But they didn't do any better than the downtown store; they only added to expenses without, it seemed, bringing in new or additional customers. DOWNTOWN went in for expensive promitions—which brought a flurry of activity for two days and then died. DOWNTOWN tried to compete with the discounters through a "Basement Store"—only to find that this downgraded its entire merchandise without bringing in a great many new sales, and so on.

For 1973, DOWNTOWN, though selling almost $75 million of merchandise, showed no profit on operations and was saved from showing a loss only by a real estate profit of $350,000 when it sold its two suburban shopping centers to a major supermarket chain.

Thereupon Fred Bohannon handed in his resignation.

No one in the five-man Executive Committee of Midwest Department Store Company's top management suggested that the resignation not be accepted. Indeed, only three months earlier, the five men had talked among themselves how they could get Bohannon to step down despite his ironclad contract.

But when the question arose whom to put into DOWNTOWN and what to do with it, the Financial Vice President, Robert Fremont, suddenly spoke up: "We'd be crazy to put a good man down there; and we'd be criminals to put a penny of additional money into DOWNTOWN. There is only one thing to do: get the hell out, fast. Let's sell the dog, or burn it down, or give it away. But let's not throw good people or good money down that bottomless well anymore. *Once a business has gone downhill as far as DOWNTOWN has*—and especially in what otherwise have been good times—*you can't save it.* The best you can expect from heroic efforts and quite improbable luck is that you can slow the drain to where you don't bleed to death right away. But you had better put your efforts and your money elsewhere—where you get results commensurate to the effort. Let's look for opportunities—there are more than we have money or men for: new shopping centers, new distribution concepts, all kinds of things, where we have a chance. I am not blaming Bohannon; he is more competent than some successful managers we have. But it's been a tough ten years; and neither Bohannon nor we apparently understand Twin Forks. Anyone who wants us to stay in there will have to convince me that there are reasons we can expect to get anything for our efforts other than further deterioration or, at best, a repetition of the last ten years. All right, we made a mistake fifteen years ago—now is our chance to get out of it."

What would you answer Fremont? What do you think of his line of reasoning?

PERFORMANCE IN THE SERVICE INSTITUTION

PART TWO

Case Number 1

The Dilemma of Aliesha State College: Competence Versus Need

Until the 1960s, Aliesha was a well-reputed, somewhat sleepy State Teachers College located on the outer fringes of a major metropolitan area. Then with the rapid expansion of college enrollments, the state converted Aliesha to a four-year state college (and the plans called for its becoming a state university with graduate work and perhaps even with a medical school in the 1980s). Within ten years, Aliesha grew from 1,500 to 9,000 students. Its budget expanded even faster than the enrollment, increasing twenty-fold during that period.

The only part of Aliesha that did not grow was the original part, the teachers' college; there enrollment actually went down. Everything else seemed to flourish. In addition to building new four-year schools of liberal arts, business, veterinary medicine, dentistry, Aliesha developed many community service programs. Among them were a rapidly growing evening program, a mental-health clinic, and a speech therapy center for children with speech defects—the only one in the area. Even within education one area grew—the demonstration high school attached to the old teacher's college. Even though it enrolled only 300 students, this high school was taught by the leading experts in teacher education and was considered the best high school in the whole area.

Then in 1976, the budget was suddenly cut quite sharply by the state legislature. At the same time the faculty demanded and got a fairly hefty raise in salary. It was clear that something had to give—the budget deficit was much too great to be covered by ordinary cost reductions. When the faculty committee sat down with the President and the Board of Trustees, two candidates for abandonment emerged after long and heated wrangling: the speech-therapy program and the demonstration high school. Both cost about the same—and both were extremely expensive.

The speech-therapy clinic, everyone agreed, addressed itself to a real need and one of high priority. But—and everybody had to agree as the evidence was overwhelming—it did not do the job. Indeed it did such a poor, sloppy, disorganized job that pediatricians, psychiatrists, and psychologists hesitated to refer their patients to the clinic. The reason was that the clinic was a college program run to teach psychology students rather than to help children with serious speech impediments.

The opposite criticism applied to the high school. No one questioned its excellence and the impact it made on the education students who listened in on its classes and on many young teachers in the area who came in as auditors. But what need did it fill? There were plenty of perfectly adequate high schools in the area.

"How can we justify," asked one of the psychologists connected with the speech clinic, "running an unnecessary high school in which each child costs as much as a graduate student at Harvard?"

"But how can we justify," asked the Dean of the School of Education, himself one of the outstanding teachers in the demonstration high school, "a speech clinic that has no results even though each of its patients costs the state as much as one of our demonstration high school students, or more?"

At this point the Chairman of the Board of Trustees took the floor. "What I hear is that the defenders of the speech clinic argue need, though they admit incompetence and inability to correct it; for state law and our charter demand that a college activity be focused on the needs of the students, which, you tell us, makes it impossible to run a therapeutically effective speech clinic. Still, you argue need. And you," he said, turning to the defenders of the demonstration high school, "argue competence. You do make a contribution—to the remaining education students but, above all, by setting standards of teaching and education that raise the level of all high schools in our area. But the need you satisfy is minor compared to the unique need the speech clinic should be satisfying but isn't. We are not allowed by state law to cut activities below the budget given to us. Otherwise I'd move that we close down *both* the speech clinic and the demonstration high school. But we have to close one. Which deserves priority: need or competence?"

Which does?

Case Number 2

What Are "Results" in the Hospitals?

Robert Armstrong joined the struggling family company when he came out of the navy after World War II. A few years later his father died suddenly and Armstrong took over what was then a very small, and indeed practically a marginal, business. For more than 20 years the business took all his time—or almost all of it. For Armstrong had always had a strong interest in health care. As a youngster he thought seriously of going to medical school and might have done so had he not been drafted while in college.He therefore began to work for one of the major community hospitals in his metropolitan area almost immediately. He was elected to the hospital's board in 1955 and became chairman of the board in 1965. Armstrong took these duties seriously and gave unstintingly of his time and energy.

By the early 1970s, the Armstrong Company had become a substantial business. Robert Armstrong, who alone had been "the management" twenty years earlier, had built what he considered an unusually competent management team. Though Armstrong was still in his early fifties, business had begun to bore him. He had also begun to resent the heavy travel schedule that the business imposed on him.

When the administrator of the hospital suddenly suffered a stroke and had to retire, the Board appointed a selection committee to choose a replacement and named Robert Armstrong chairman. Before the first meeting of the committee, Armstrong met with the hospital's Chief of Medical Services—a respected physician who had also for many years been Armstrong's personal doctor—to decide with him what kind of a man the committee should be looking for. To Armstrong's total surprise, the doctor said, "Look, Bob, cut out the nonsense. You don't have to look for the man to head up St. Luke's. You are the man. No one knows more about the place than you do. No one is better accepted. And I know—you told me so last October at your annual physical—that your present job bores you, that they don't need you in the company anymore, and that you and Libby are tired of your eternal traveling. All right, so you are making a great deal more dough as president of Armstrong than we pay a hospital administrator. But you have enough money and don't need a big income. Hospital administrators aren't that badly paid. They make as much as you pay your vice presidents—at least that's what you told us when we last raised the administrator's salary in the board meeting six months ago."

The more Armstrong thought about this, the more sense it made to him. But also, the more he thought, the more uneasy he became about his ability to do the job. He went back to the doctor and said: "If I take this job, how do I measure my performance? What results should I be after? What is performance in a hospital, and what are results?"

The doctor grinned broadly and said: "I knew you'd ask those questions and that's why I'd love to see you take the job. I know what results are in my work and in my practice. But neither I nor anyone else knows what they are for the hospital. Maybe it's time some disagreeable type like you asks these questions."

Armstrong took the job and soon became known as one of the most effective and accomplished hospital managers in the country. Six years later the American College of Hospital Administrators named him Hospital Administrator of the Year. In his short acceptance speech Armstrong said: "To take the job as hospital administrator was the most intelligent thing I did in my whole life—it's been a wonderful six years. But the one question I came in to answer, I still can't answer. In fact, I am more confused now than I was six years ago. I know now that a modern big-city hospital has a multitude of objectives and serves a multitude of customers and clients: the doctors who look upon the hospital as an extension of their practice; the patients, who expect us to cure them or at least not to harm them; their families; the community; the various agencies—governments, Blue Cross, insurance companies, employers, unions and so on—who pay our bills; and many others. I know that we are expected to remedy damage that has already been done, the one job we are reasonably good at. But we are increasingly expected to be the community's health care center and to help keep healthy people healthy. Increasingly we are expected to substitute for the private physician in treating the poor, especially in the inner city.

"I have given up the hope of finding one performance goal and one performance measurement. But what bothers me is that I really don't know how to measure performance in any single one of these missions. I do not know how to define what is 'good performance' in any area, what to strive for, what to give priority to, and what to abandon or play down. With eight percent of the country's national product going to health care—and the cost going up—health care is too important not to have objectives, performance standards, and measurements. But can any one of you experienced hospital administrators in the audience tell me what objectives, goals, standards and measurements you are using or which ones I might try using?"

Is there any way to tackle Armstrong's question, or is "health care" so intangible as to defy definitions, objectives, and measurement?

Case Number 3

The University Art Museum: Defining Purpose and Mission

Visitors to the campus were always shown the University Art Museum, of which the large and distinguished university was very proud. A photograph of the handsome neoclassical building that housed the Museum had long been used by the university for the cover of its brochures and catalogues.

The building, together with a substantial endowment, was given to the university around 1912 by an alumnus, the son of the university's first president, who had become very wealthy as an investment banker. He also gave the university his own small, but high quality, collections—one of Etruscan figurines, and one, unique in America, of English pre-Raphaelite paintings. He then served as the Museum's unpaid director until his death. During his tenure he brought a few additional collections to the museum, largely from other alumni of the university. Only rarely did the museum purchase anything. As a result, the museum housed several small collections of uneven quality. As long as the founder ran the museum, none of the collections was ever shown to anybody except a few members of the university's art history faculty, who were admitted as the founder's private guests.

After the founder's death, in the late 1920s, the university intended to bring in a professional museum director. Indeed, this had been part of the agreement under which the founder had given the museum. A search committee was to be appointed, but in the meantime a graduate student in art history who had shown interest in the museum and who had spent a good many hours in it, took over temporarily. At first, she did not even have a title, let alone a salary. But she stayed on acting as the museum's director and over the next 30 years was promoted in stages to that title. But from the first day, whatever her title, she was in charge. She immediately set about changing the museum altogether. She catalogued the collections. She pursued new gifts, again primarily small collections from alumni and other friends of the university. She organized fund raising for the museum. But, above all, she began to integrate the museum into the work of the university. When a space problem arose in the years immediately following World War II, Miss Kirkhoff offered the third floor of the museum to the art history faculty, which moved its offices there. She remodeled the building to include classrooms and a modern and well-appointed auditorium. She raised funds to build one of the best research and reference libraries in art history in the country. She also began to organize a series of special exhibitions built around one of the museum's own collections, complemented by loans from outside collections. For each of these exhibitions she had a distinguished member of the university's art faculty write a catalogue. These catalogues speedily became the leading scholarly texts in the fields.

Miss Kirkhoff ran the University Art Museum for almost half a century. But old age ultimately defeated her. At the age of 68 after suffering a severe stroke, she had to retire. In her letter of resignation she proudly pointed to the museum's growth and accomplishment under her stewardship. "Our endowment," she wrote, "now compares favorably with museums several times our size. We never have had to ask the university for any money other than for our share of the university's insurance policies. Our collections in the areas of our strength, while small, are of first-rate quality and importance. Above all, we are being used by more people than any museum of our size. Our lecture series, in which members of the university's art history faculty present a major subject to a university audience of students and faculty, attract regularly three to five hundred people; and if we had the seating capacity, we could easily have a larger audience. Our exhibitions are seen and studied by more visitors, most of them members of the university community, than all but the most highly publicized exhibitions in the very big museums ever draw. Above all, the courses and seminars offered in the museum have become one of the most popular and most rapidly growing educational features of the university. No other museum in this country or anywhere else," concluded Miss Kirkhoff, "has so successfully integrated art into the life of a major university and a major university into the work of a museum."

Miss Kirkhoff strongly recommended that the university bring in a professional museum director as her successor. "The museum is much too big and much too important to be entrusted to another amateur such as I was forty-five years ago", she wrote. "And it needs careful thinking regarding its direction, its basis of support and its future relationship with the university."

The university took Miss Kirkhoff's advice. A search committee was duly appointed and, after one year's work, it produced a candidate whom everybody approved. The candidate was himself a graduate of the university who had then obtained his Ph.D. in art history and in museum work from the university. Both his teaching and administrative record were sound, leading to his present museum directorship in a medium-sized city. There he converted an old, well-known, but rather sleepy museum to a lively, community-oriented museum whose exhibitions were well publicized and attracted large crowds.

The new museum director took over with great fanfare in September, 1971. Less than three years later he left—with less fanfare, but still with considerable noise. Whether he resigned or was fired was not quite clear. But that there was bitterness on both sides was only too obvious.

The new director, upon his arrival, had announced that he looked upon the museum as a "major community resource" and intended to "make the tremendous artistic and scholarly resources of the Museum fully available to the academic community as well as to the public." When he said these things in an interview with the college newspaper, everybody nodded in approval. It soon became clear that what he meant by "community resource" and what the faculty and students understood by these words were not the same. The museum had always been "open to the public" but, in practice, it was members of the college community who used the museum and attended its lectures, its exhibitions, and its frequent seminars.

The first thing the new director did, however, was to promote visits from the public schools in the area. He soon began to change the exhibition policy. Instead of organizing small shows, focused on a major collection of the museum and built around a scholarly catalogue, he began to organize "popular exhibitions" around "topics of general interest" such as "Women Artists through the Ages." He promoted these exhibitions vigorously in the newspapers, in radio and television interviews and, above all, in the local schools. As a result, what had been a busy but quiet place was soon knee-deep in school children, taken to the museum in special buses which cluttered the access roads around the museum and throughout the campus. The faculty, which was not particularly happy with the resulting noise and confusion, became thoroughly upset when the scholarly old chairman of the art history department was mobbed by fourth-graders who sprayed him with their water pistols as he tried to push his way through the main hall to his office.

Increasingly, the new director did not design his own shows, but brought in traveling exhibitions from major museums, importing their catalogue as well rather than have his own faculty produce one.

The students too were apparently unenthusiastic after the first six or eight months, during which the new director had been somewhat of a campus hero. Attendance at the classes and seminars held in the art museum fell off sharply, as did attendance at the evening lectures. When the editor of the campus newspaper interviewed students for a story on the museum, he was told again and again that the museum had become too noisy and too "sensational" for students to enjoy the classes and to have a chance to learn.

What brought all this to a head was an Islamic art exhibit in late 1973. Since the museum had little Islamic art, nobody criticized the showing of a traveling exhibit, offered on very advantageous terms with generous financial assistance from some of the Arab governments. But then, instead of inviting one of the University's own faculty members to deliver the customary talk at the opening of the exhibit, the director brought in a cultural attache of one of the Arab embassies in Washington. The speaker, it was reported, used the occasion to deliver a violent attack on Israel and on the American policy of supporting Israel against the Arabs. A week later, the university senate decided to appoint an advisory committee, drawn mostly from members of the art history faculty, which, in the future, would have to approve all plans for exhibits and lectures. The director thereupon, in an interview with the campus newspaper sharply attacked the faculty as "elitist" and "snobbish" and as believing that "art belongs to the rich." Six months later, in June, 1974, his resignation was announced.

Under the bylaws of the university, the academic senate appoints a search committee. Normally, this is pure formality. The chairman of the appropriate department submits the department's nominees for the committee who are approved and appointed, usually without debate. But when the academic senate early the following semester was asked to appoint the search committee, things were far from "normal." The Dean who presided, sensing the tempers in the room, tried to smooth over things by saying, "Clearly, we picked the wrong person the last time. We will have to try very hard to find the right one this time."

He was immediately interrupted by an economist, known for his populism, who broke in and said, "I admit that the late director was probably not the right personality. But I strongly believe that his personality was not at the root of the problem. He tried to do what needs doing and this got him in trouble with the faculty. He tried to make our museum a community resource, to bring in the community and to make art accessible to broad masses of people, to the blacks and the Puerto Ricans, to the kids from the ghetto schools and to a lay public. And this is what we really resented. Maybe his methods were not the most tactful ones—I admit I could have done without those interviews he gave. But what he tried to do was right. We had better commit ourselves to the policy he wanted to put into effect, or else we will have deserved his attacks on us as 'elitist' and 'snobbish.' "

"This is nonsense," cut in the usually silent and polite senate member from the art history faculty. "It makes absolutely no sense for our museum to try to become the kind of community resource our late director and my distinguished colleague want it to be. First there is no need. The city has one of the world's finest and biggest museums and it does exactly that and does it very well. Secondly, we here have neither the artistic resources nor the financial resources to serve the community at large. We can do something different but equally important and indeed unique. Our is the only museum in the country, and perhaps in the world, that is fully integrated with an academic community and truly a teaching institution. We are using it, or at least we used to until the last few unfortunate years, as a major educational resource for all our students. No other museum in the country, and as far as I know in the world, is bringing undergraduates into art the way we do. All of us, in addition to our scholarly and graduate work, teach undergraduate courses for people who are not going to be art majors or art historians. We work with the engineering students and show them what we do in our conservation and restoration work. We work with architecture students and show them the development of architecture through the ages. Above all, we work with liberal arts students, who often have had no exposure to art before they came here and who enjoy our courses all the more because they are scholarly and not just 'art appreciation.' This is unique and this is what our museum can do and should do."

"I doubt that this is really what we should be doing," commented the chairman of the mathematics department. "The museum, as far as I know, is part of the graduate faculty. It should concentrate on training art historians in its Ph.D. program, on its scholarly work and on its research. I would strongly urge that the museum be considered an adjunct to graduate and especially to Ph.D. education, confine itself to this work, and stay out of all attempts to be 'popular', both on campus and outside of it. The glory of the museum is the scholarly catalogues produced by our faculty, and our Ph.D. graduates who are sought after by art history faculties throughout the country. This is the museum's mission, which can only be impaired by the attempt to be 'popular', whether with students or with the public".

"These are very interesting and important comments", said the Dean, still trying to pacify. "But I think this can wait until we know who the new director is going to be. Then we should raise these questions with him."

"I beg to differ, Mr. Dean," said one of the elder statesmen of the faculty. "During the summer months, I discussed this question with an old friend and neighbor of mine in the country, the director of one of the nation's great museums. He said to me: 'You do not have a personality problem, you have a *management* problem. You have not, as a university, taken responsibility for the mission, the direction, and the objectives of your museum. Until you do this, no director can succeed. And this is *your* decision. In fact, you cannot hope to get a good man until you can tell him what your basic objectives are. If your late director is to blame—I know him and I know that he is abrasive—it is for being willing to take on a job when you, the university, had not faced up to the basic management decisions. There is no point talking about *who* should manage until it is clear *what* it is that has to be managed and for what.' "

At this point the dean realized that he had to adjourn the discussion unless he wanted the meeting to degenerate into a brawl. But he also realized that he had to identify the issues and possible decisions before the next faculty meeting a month later. Here is the list of questions he put down on paper later that evening:

1. What are the possible purposes of the University Museum:
    ——to serve as a laboratory for the graduate art-history faculty and the doctoral students in the field?
    to serve as major "enrichment" for the undergraduate who is not an art-history student but wants both a "liberal education" and a counterweight to the highly bookish diet fed to him in most of our courses?
    ——to serve the metropolitan community—and especially its schools—outside the campus gates?

2. Who are or should be its customers?
    ——the graduate students in professional training to be teachers of art history?
    ——the undergraduate community—or rather, the entire college community?
    ——the metropolitan community and especially the teachers and youngsters in the public schools?
    ——any others?

3. Which of these purposes are compatible and could be served simultaneously? Which are mutually exclusive or at the very least are likely to get into each other's way?

4. What implications for the structure of the museum, the qualifications of its director and its relationship to the university follow from each of the above purposes?

5. Do we need to find out more about the needs and wants of our various potential customers to make

an intelligent policy decision? How could we go about it?

The dean distributed these questions to the members of the faculty with the request that they think them through and discuss them before the next meeting of the academic senate.

How would you tackle these questions? And are they the right questions?

Case Number 4

What is Our Mission?
What is Our Market?

The Worldwide Youth Exchange Federation grew out of talks a group of young returning GIs had during the long ride back home from occupied Germany on a troop ship in the spring of 1946. These young men were all veterans of the American Ambulance Corps who had enlisted for non-combat duty with the British before the U.S. entered the war. After Pearl Harbor, they were transferred to the American forces. Bedell Smith, General Eisenhower's Chief of Staff, heard of them and attached them to his own office, where they served as advance scouts for the relief needs of liberated territory, first in Italy and then in France, and finally in Germany and Austria. These young men—most of whom had been university students who enlisted—began to talk among themselves of their experiences. They inevitably raised the question: "What can we do to prevent a recurrence? What can we do to make peace more secure?" They decided that what was needed was understanding among the peoples of different nations, and that such understanding would have to begin with the young. Accordingly, after they got home they began to organize—at first completely at random—exchanges of high school students, under which Americans of high school age would go to Europe, stay with a European family and go to school in Europe for a year; in turn, a European high school

35

youngster would come to this country, stay with an American family and attend an American high school for one year. The idea was an almost immediate success and other GIs picked it up and began to work on it in their own communities. And soon there was need for an organization. In 1950, by which time the annual volume of student exchange between the United States and Europe and between Europe and the United States already exceeded two hundred students each way, the Worldwide Youth Exchange Federation was started with a small grant from a major foundation and with one full-time employee. Since then the organization has grown steadily, year by year, until by 1975 it was sending three thousand American high school students abroad each year, mostly still to Europe but also to South America, Japan, and Indonesia. It was bringing roughly the identical number of high school students from overseas to the United States for a stay in an American home and for attendance for one year at an American high school. By 1975 the staff numbered almost 140 professionals, of whom about 80 were stationed in the United States.

In 1975 a young man took over as the new Chief Executive—the first to succeed the original administrator who had started in 1950. Hugh Williamson was barely 30 when he took over. In his junior year in high school he had himself been one of the students under the Worldwide Youth Exchange Federation program; he had spent a happy year in France, with a French family and in a French school. He had then gone to the State University in his native Wisconsin, obtained a Ph.D. in Psychology, and joined the State Department as an educational specialist, in which capacity he had worked in several South American countries. When he returned to a job with a big American company, he found himself rather bored and was therefore delighted when offered the job of President of Worldwide Youth Exchange Federation.

However, he was appalled by what he found. The staff seemed to him to be large beyond any need and totally disorganized. The finances were chaotic, to say the least. No one really knew how much it cost to bring a student to this country or to send one abroad. No one seemed to know who was responsible for budgets, for raising money, or for authorizing expenditures. There was also total confusion regarding the relationship between the paid staff and volunteers. In the United States most of the work was done by local chapters run by volunteers, in most cases still the former GIs who had first given birth to the idea. Overseas there were paid country representatives. There were, however, no local chapters. Overseas students returning from the United States—eighteen year olds—were expected to do what legwork was needed in their communities, both to recruit applicants for student exchange and, more important, to find families willing to receive an American student for one year.

Williamson spent almost two years straightening out administration, slimming the staff in New York, where little work was actually being done (though voluminous records were being kept). Actually, he found the organization to be fundamentally very healthy, or so it seemed by the yardsticks which Worldwide Youth Exchange Federation had always applied to its own results—that is, by the number of people who were applying for participation in this program. In 1976 25,000 Americans applied to go abroad and 25,000 students in foreign countries applied for a year in the U.S.—about 18,000 of them Europeans and 5,000 Latin Americans. And better than one out of every ten applicants—3,000 Americans and 3,000 foreigners—could actually be placed. Equally satisfactory, at least at first glance, was the performance record, as measured by the traditional yardstick of the number of students who completed their exchange year. The drop-out rate remained well below five percent. The great majority of students (93 percent) and the great majority of hosts, both in the United States and abroad, expressed themselves as very satisfied with their experiences.

Yet the more Williamson dug, the more uneasy did he become. He saw financial trouble ahead. For the first time, the true costs of the exchange were known, and they turned out to be very high indeed. The host family, of course, contributed the support of their guest—so there was no need to raise that money. The schools that participated, mostly public high schools or their equivalent abroad, contributed a free place. But even so, each student cost almost $2,000 including his transportation, his counselling, and so on. Particularly disturbing to Williamson was the fact that the entire financial burden was being borne by the American chapters. As he traveled through the United States and visited the chapters, he heard more and more complaints about this inequity. Why should the whole burden of the program be borne by the Americans while the Europeans and Japanese, though equally able to pay their share of the costs, did not contribute a penny? Even more disturbing, as he reflected on his frequent trips about the country, was the fact that the chapters, practically without exception, depended on people who were aging, namely the original founders. More and more of the former beneficiaries of the program—that is former exchange students—were reaching the age at which they should take over the responsibility for the organization. But by and large they were being kept out of the organization's affairs, or at least not actively recruited. In Europe, he found that the returning students, who were very enthusiastic at first and willing to work hard, soon went off to the university and disappeared from the organization's view. No adults in the respective communities and very few of the host families had been organized to support the Federation activities and to do the work. Finally, he became disturbed by hearing from chapter after chapter and in foreign country after foreign country that host families no longer were standing in line to get high school students from abroad. On the contrary, they had to be convinced that they would not be saddled with a young "hippie" with long and filthy hair, dirty and torn blue-jeans, who were smoking pot and sleeping around. Although the students, of whom Williamson saw a great deal, were almost the opposite of that type—and sometimes shocked him by being utterly "square" and ultra-serious—he realized that teenagers from abroad were no longer automatically welcome everywhere.

Williamson formulated in his own mind what he considered the key questions: the sources of finance; the organization of the chapters and their staffing; and the building of a permanent, self-perpetuating volunteer organization abroad. He also felt that he needed to recruit a board of nationally known names—if only to help him raise money. When he had formulated these questions, he went to an older friend of his family, a highly successful corporation lawyer in his native Wisconsin, whose advice and counsel he had repeatedly sought in the past. The old friend received him most cordially and listened attentively, asking all kinds of questions. Then he said: "I have been listening to you for an entire day. I am totally confused as to what you think the mission of the Worldwide Youth Exchange Federation is and where you see its market. Who are your customers? And why do they 'buy' from you?

What is your 'product'? Before you have answered these questions, all the rest are meaningless."

How would you go about answering these questions? Do you think, by the way, that they need to be answered first or that Williamson, with his focus on specifics, is more likely to succeed?

Case Number 5

The Future of
Mt. Hillyer College

The 150-year-celebrations at Mt. Hillyer College had gone off without a hitch. They had come to an end a few hours earlier when, after giving the Commencement Speech and receiving an honorary doctorate, the President of the United States had taken off in Air Force One. Soon students, parents, and guests had followed him. And now, in the long twilight hours of a beautiful June evening, Mt. Hillyer College was again quiet. But there were still a few people in the President's House, sitting on the porch and relaxing from a strenuous week. They were the people who, for a whole year, had worked on the Anniversary week: the President of the College, Dr. Leonides, a young, energetic man and his wife, the head of the Psychology Department; the President Emeritus, old Dr. Langton who had built Mt. Hillyer into its present size, eminence, and prosperity after he took over a sleepy small school right after World War II; the Chairwoman of the Board of Trustees, Judge Catherine Holman of the State's Supreme Court and the College's most distinguished living graduate; her husband, the Dean of the State University's prestigious Law School; the Dean of the Faculty; the Dean of Students; and a few other senior administrators and the Student Body President. The President Emeritus, as was his wont, went around the group asking them what each thought had been the most important happening of the week. Finally he turned to the chairwoman's husband, the Law School Dean, and said: "Dean Holman, you are the only outsider here; yet you haven't said a word. What do you consïder the most important or most interesting event of the last week?" Holman smiled and said: "You know to me the most interesting thing was something that did NOT happen. Everybody talked about the past of Mt. Hillyer, its accomplishments, its many firsts, its glories. No one talked about the future. To be sure, we had a good talk on the Future of Liberal Education—witty, erudite, inspirational. But it really only told us that liberal education is good. Mt. Hillyer is a pretty big place by now, at least for a private undergraduate school. Thanks mainly to the two of you, Dr. Langton and Dr. Leonides, it now has 4,500 students. When my wife went here, you had no more than 450 to 500. It has a name and a reputation and a good endowment for its size. But what is its excellence going to be tomorrow? Or doesn't it need such a thing? Can it be content with being like every one else, only a little more so? In a law school we know—or think we do—what we are trying to do. And while the number of graduates who pass the Bar Examination is hardly a good measurement, at least it is a measurement. I know there are some attractive features to Mt. Hillyer—it's lovely country out there. But is that enough? The people who started and built Mt. Hillyer—we heard a lot about them these last few days—wouldn't have thought so. They had a goal when they started a school in what was then a God-forsaken wilderness on the very edge of the beyond. And their successors, who in the late nineteenth century cut the college loose from church affiliation, went co-educational, and pushed science and government and economics, also had a pretty clear idea of what the college was supposed to stand for. I don't expect you to come up with answers. But I am a little disturbed that no one this past week has been asking any questions. Most of the work of higher education in this country is already being done in large, urban mass institutions, tax-supported. Is it enough for Mt. Hillyer to be small, private (and thereby expensive) and still semi-rural? Or do you have to stand for something in higher education? Should it be excellence in teaching? Should it be leadership in new areas of learning and knowledge? Should it be close integration with the world of work, the adult world which students as a rule know nothing of—for instance through an organized work program for students during three months of the year? Or is it enough to try to get a few faculty members with big reputations and then to be selective in admitting students who have both the money and the grades? But," said Dean Holman, "my real concern is how one asks these questions—or perhaps my real concern is that we in higher education don't ask them, as a rule but make instead speeches about the glories of liberal education."

Are these legitimate concerns, do you think? And can one come to grips with them—or can one only make speeches about them?

Case Number 6

Cost Control
in the Hospital

It took only ten days for Seymour Politz to get the following reply to the letter he had sent to his cousin Linda:

> Dear Seymour:
> I am delighted to give you my opinion of the expansion plans for Glen River Hospital, of which you are Chairman of the Finance Committee (which I didn't know). I am impressed by your excellent planning. Indeed, I intend to use your projections of population trends in relation to hospital needs as the model for my staff here. We are just about to develop guide lines for hospital planning for our state, so Glen River's plans are coming in very handy indeed. And please give Dr. Bernauer, your Administrator, my best regards and my compliments on an excellent job of planning. I knew the plans would be a model the moment I saw his name on them; I remember vividly the contribution he made when he and I sat together on President Nixon's Committee on Military Hospitals.
> I do indeed agree with Dr. Bernauer's conclusion that Glen River Hospital needs urgently to add some 30 rooms—or sixty beds—and that what you need are additional clinical-care beds. As a matter of fact, I think that your figures are low; with your population forecasts for the Glen River area, you might better aim at a minimum of 75 new clinical beds, or around 38 or 40 semi-

private rooms. But, Seymour, you do have these rooms. Or rather you are today using some 40 clinical—and that means high-cost—rooms for purposes that require only much cheaper facilities—cheaper by two thirds or so in respect to capital investment, cheaper by about one half in respect to service, and cheaper also in respect to maintenance.

You have in your main hospital building clinical care rooms reserved for maternity. Childbirth is not a disease; all the healthy mother needs is a place to lie down and sleep off the fatigue. And she should move around, have something to do. In other words, what she needs is the simplest kind of motel room, preferably with a day bed she can open or close as she wants. Some babies do need a clinical-care facility, but that's a small room and a simple one. Mothers need a place to make coffee, to sit down and to chat. And the cost of the kind of rooms you need for mothers—including an intensive-care facility for infants in trouble, delivery rooms and recovery rooms—is around one third the cost of the intensive-care rooms. Build a motel for maternity, and free the maternity rooms you now use for clinical-care patients. Similarly you have 10 rooms for mental patients—and you don't admit any serious cases. You admit people with depressions, people with anxieties, people who need counselling or protection against a demanding world. They should be forced to move around, eat in a cafeteria, see other people—again a small motel with some extra rooms for counselling and group therapy is what you need, rather than clinical rooms. Finally you are using 15 rooms—perhaps more—for surgical patients, especially in orthopedic surgery and orthopedic treatment such as traction for people with serious back pain. This does not require clinical care. The person who has had ankle surgery is kept in the hospital only because the cast shouldn't dry too fast—so he stays three days until he can put weight on the cast. The woman with a bad back needs traction six or ten hours a day for two or three days—but she doesn't need clinical care; she needs a bed to lie on with the leg in the air. You do need operating rooms for these patients (you plan on five additional ones anyhow); you do need a recovery room; and you do need a hospital-type bed to make it easier for the nurse. But you do not need the expensive clinical-care hospital room. You need something quite simple and much cheaper.

So I advise that you re-draw your plans and build a 35-to 40-room two-story motel—70 to 80 beds on a semi-private basis—at the lowest possible cost. I estimate it at around 40 percent of what you have budgeted for your expansion. And that should include the cost of refurbishing the 42-bed clinical rooms you now misuse for maternity, mental patients, and surgical recovery into the clinical-care rooms you need—that would give you all you need and a little more at much less cost; yet you'd have better facilities.

One more thing, Seymour. Your plan proposes to raise all the money Glen River Hospital needs through a fund raising campaign and as charitable contributions. That's folly and vanity. It costs much too much. In such a campaign, thirty cents or so of every dollar raised is spent on campaign costs. And then half the people who promise to give are never heard from. The only sensible way—and the only cheap one—is to borrow commercially as much as you can. You should be able to get 90 percent of your needs from banks, insurance companies, the dormitory authority of your state, Uncle Sam, and so on—and at reasonable interest rates. After all, ninety percent of your cost is underwritten by insurance companies, Blue Cross, and the government. The last 10 percent—that's what one uses philanthropy for. To use it for anything else cannot be justified in today's hospital.

Give my love to Kathy-Ann; tell her we already look forward to your visit this fall. And Jim wants me to tell you that he expects you to have a few days to go fishing with him. He has invented a new fly he is most eager to show off to you. Until then

As always yours,

Signed: Linda Politz Buxbaum M.D.
Associate Commissioner of
Hospitals
State of   ....

Seymour Politz was delighted—the letter confirmed the hunch that led him to write to Linda in the first place. When he received Dr. Bernauer's proposal for expanding Glen River Hospital two weeks ago, he was quite upset. The proposal called for three times as much money as he had anticipated. He himself had intended to contribute heavily. But although he was a fairly wealthy man, the projected costs were many times what he could contribute. To raise that large a sum through a fund drive seemed to him almost impossible, especially with the concern in the town of Glen River over rising hospital costs. But 40 percent of the amount proposed—and most of it borrowed from the banks—that would be no problem. He himself could surely make up the difference between what the banks would lend and what would be needed.

And so he went to see Dr. Bernauer at the hospital. "Yes," said Bernauer, "I know all this—though your cousin, as usual, is a little quicker than most of us are. But, Seymour, it won't work even though it makes sense. The other trustees are never going to agree to borrowing from the banks and insurance companies at commercial rates. They'll tell you that once you do this you can't raise money any more through a charity drive—people will say 'if they can get money from the banks, why should I *give*?' I think the trustees are wrong—people are a little brighter than that. But you'll see that they will flatly refuse to do anything but pass the hat, no matter how expensive it is. But your greatest obstacle," said the Administrator, "will be the physicians. Maybe some of the surgeons will go along. There are now a few free-standing surgical clinics run on the same principle, although all of them are profit-making ventures and I haven't heard of surgeons in non-profit community hospitals like ours accepting the idea of a semi-ambulatory and cheap surgical facility. But the obstetricians and the psychiatrists and the psychologists are going to yell bloody murder. You are down-grading them and their skill; if their patients aren't truly 'very sick' people, then they won't be respected as true healers."

Politz didn't believe the Administrator. But a few talks—with fellow trustees, with the chief of obstetrics and the chief of psychiatry—and he learned that the Administrator was right. So, downcast, he went back to Dr. Bernauer and asked "Is there anything we can do?" "Oh sure," said Bernauer, "sell the hospital to a profit-making hospital corporation or convert it into a profit-making hospital owned by our doctors; and, presto, there won't be any trouble." "You are a cynic," said Politz. "No, I don't think so," said Bernauer. "Sure, some doctors are too greedy. But the profits they'd make as owners of Glen River Hospital are so trivial as to make no difference to any of them. And it isn't *their* profits that would make them change their minds anyhow. What your cousin Linda recommends is being done the other end of the metropolitan area at St. Vincent's, which the nuns sold to a hospital-company in

St. Louis last year. There the doctors accept and support it, even though they have no share in the ownership and in any profits. I have been thinking about this for a long time," said Bernauer. "It bothers me. I think I can explain it. In a community non-profit hospital like ours, low costs and efficiency aren't values. The trustees glory in the good cause and are really upset if you point out that we are very much like a business or should be. Why should they then sit on the board and give of their time and money? And the physicians are much too far away from financial results. If they own the hospital, they see revenues as meaningful. If a company owns it, they respect—maybe over-respect—the businessman. But if it's a community hospital and a good cause, well, you don't put a price tag on good works. . . . "

What do you think of Dr. Bernauer's explanation? And by the way, could Politz and Bernauer do anything to change the attitude and point of view of the trustees and the physicians? And if they have no success—and few attempts of this kind have been successful—should they go ahead with building the very expensive clinical-care beds and with raising the money through an extremely expensive, if not wasteful, fund-raising campaign? Or should they instead try to have their state develop regulatory rules?

PRODUCTIVE WORK AND ACHIEVING WORKER

PART THREE

Can One LEARN
to Manage Subordinates?

Tom McAvoy was 27 and three years out of law school when he entered the legal department of Electro-Magnetic Induction Technology Industries as a legal researcher on an antitrust case. The company then had about fifty million dollars in sales and operated almost exclusively in North America—and really only in the USA as the Canadian affiliate was barely more than a sales office. By the time McAvoy was 45, he was Associate General Counsel of a company—now renamed Emitco—with sales of 750 million dollars and major operations in all developed countries, and especially in the European Common Market, where one-third of the company's sales now originated. McAvoy's father had been a diplomat, and Tom had spent much of his childhood and youth abroad before coming home to the U.S. for college and law school. He therefore was multilingual with excellent French, German and Spanish and adequate Italian. Negotiations and legal work in Europe thus naturally had gravitated to him. He had become the company's mainstay in the development of the European network of Emitco subsidiaries and affiliates, was a member of the management committee of Emitco-Europe, and spent about half of his time in Europe and on European business.

It was no secret to any one in Emitco that McAvoy wanted to live in Europe. When he suggested establishing the company's European headquarters in Paris, more than one wit in the company commented that McAvoy's love for that city was the real reason for the choice. When therefore the company's vice president-European informed headquarters that he intended to retire on his sixtieth birthday, nine months hence, McAvoy's choice as his successor surprised no one. And it pleased the heads of the European companies who had worked closely with McAvoy over the years and had found him intelligent, well-informed and distinctly *simpatico*—whereas they often had difficulties working with some of the others in Emitco headquarters—most of them small-town midwesterners who had never lived outside their own country.

McAvoy was elated, but he also worried. He was conscious of the fact that he had never before managed people—he had always been a staff specialist. And now he was going to have reporting to him nine line managers and a total of 19,000 people in nine different European countries. He therefore requested a three-month leave— ostensibly to get his teenaged children into boarding schools and to move his home to Paris, but in reality to prepare himself for line operating responsibility. Being a conscientious man he got a list—a very long list—of books on personnel management and read them all. But the more he read, the more confused he became. The books were full of procedures, but McAvoy was fully determined to leave procedures to the personnel department. Otherwise they all talked of the kind of man he should be or should become. But what was he supposed to *do*? He knew that he had to establish himself fairly fast—he had seen enough men get a promotion to know that one had to establish himself in a new job within a few months or so. He knew that the only aspect of the job that was new to him was managing people—but it was *totally* new to him. And he felt strongly that he had to know in advance what to do and what not to do; he knew that improvisation wasn't his way of doing things.

Finally, with most of the three months of his leave used up, he reluctantly went for advice and counsel to the retired chairman of the Emitco board, the man who had originally hired him. At the time Jonathan Forbes was an executive vice president. He had then soon become president and chief executive officer and the main architect of Emitco's growth and expansion. Forbes had never been the kind of "boss" the books recommended; he had been austere, aloof, demanding, critical, and rather distant. But McAvoy had respected him and so had many others in Emitco. And Emitco's growth and success, McAvoy believed, was primarily the result of Forbes' management of people—he seemed to be able to make the most diverse people perform and pull together.

Forbes was at first cool when McAvoy sought him out in his retirement retreat in Colorado Springs. But he warmed when McAvoy explained why he had come. "That you worry, Tom, is in itself a very good sign," Forbes said, "and perhaps it's the only thing needed to make you do a good job. Managing people isn't that hard—if you know that it is your job and that it is work. The only thing that is truly important is . . .

How would you finish the sentence? And what would you say to defend your choice of the *one* thing that is "truly important" in managing people?

Case Number 2

How to Staff the Dead-End Job

The worst labor relations in the retail business were for a long time those of one of the country's best-known department-store chains. Headquartered in the eastern United States, the chain had in the late 1920s pioneered college recruiting amid great fanfare and a good deal of favorable publicity. By 1950 or so it had become apparent that college recruiting had not only not produced the desired crop of outstanding executives. It had produced truly horrible labor relations, with wild-cat strikes being pulled all the time, with tremendous bitterness between management and employees, and with a militant union that seemed determined to drive the company out of business altogether.

It was not difficult for a new personnel director, hired to change what had become an intolerable situation, to figure out what had gone wrong—half a dozen interviews with older employees and he had the answer. While college recruitment had been started in the 1920s, it had really been pushed in the Depression years and especially by the chain's first woman executive—the personnel director during the late thirties. Herself a graduate of one of the prestigious eastern women's colleges, a high government official in the early New Deal days, and chairman of the board of trustees of her alma mater, this personnel director had gone all out to provide jobs for women college graduates, and especially for graduates of the leading eastern women's schools, at a time when jobs for anyone—let alone for young women—were exceedingly scarce. She had sent recruiters to the campuses with instructions to look for the top students and especially for those who combined academic achievement with good looks. She then brought the women to company headquarters, put them through a three-day round of interviews with the top brass and a one-day "executive aptitude test." The "winners" were hired and put to work in the stock room "to learn the business." But since there are few promotional opportunities in retail selling—at least not above the selling floor—not many were ever promoted out of the stock room, and even fewer were promoted beyond sales clerk. Most of the women escaped through marriage, but that made the ones who stayed on all the more bitter, made them feel all the more betrayed.

The new personnel director knew that he could not undo the damage, but he resolved not to continue to inflict it. He agreed that the stockroom job is the right place to begin in a department store, but at the same time, for most who work there it is almost certain to be a dead-end job. There just aren't many jobs on higher levels available. He thought through what could be done and came up with three possible answers. One was to adjust hiring to the reality of the stockroom job. He could look for new employees with limited education and limited intelligence to whom a stock-room job would present a genuine challenge and the—rare—opportunity to be advanced to salesclerk a genuine opportunity. The second approach he proposed was to keep on recruiting bright and presentable top-ranking college graduates but to make sure that those for whom promotional opportunities could not be found within the company would be placed systematically in well-paid and attractive managerial jobs with other and especially smaller stores. Finally in his most radical proposal, he recommended changing the organization so that stock-room people would have responsibility for inventory control and inventory keeping and for the merchandise displays in the store.

Every one of his proposals was immediately shot down by higher management. "All our department heads and buyers," top management said, "have started in the stock-room. Unless we hire the ablest and most promising beginners into the stock-room, we won't have any management ten or fifteen years from now. And to *place* people we have trained with the competition! That's unthinkable. And surely," top management said, "you can't be serious about giving stock clerks responsibility that properly belongs to store managers and buyers."

Can you think of any way in which to convince top management of the merits of each proposed alternative? Are there any others, by the way, which would make it possible to staff these dead-end jobs and yet give achievement and satisfaction?

Case Number 3

The New Training Director
in the Hospital

American hospitals are required by law to have a training director on staff to organize training for all employees other than medical staff who have their own training system. At first training was confined to nurses. And the training director, while now supposed to direct the training of all groups, is still almost always an experienced senior nurse. In many hospitals the training director has found the job difficult and frustrating. Even if there is money available, there usually isn't much time. And the other groups—x-ray technicians, medical technologists, physical therapists, social workers and psychiatric case workers, dieticians and all the many groups who work in the office or in housekeeping and maintenance—tend to resent the interference of an "outsider," in their areas. It is therefore by no means uncommon for a training director to resign in total frustration.

And this is what happened twice in quick succession at Metropolitan Community Hospital.

Before the administrator appointed a third training director, he thought it advisable to consult an expert in training at the local university. He wanted a training program: what courses should the hospital organize, what methods whould it employ, and how could it use existing training facilities in the area's colleges and universities? The training specialist listened politely for an hour and then said, "I don't know much about hospitals—only what I learned as a patient, and fortunately my experience as such is very limited. But I think I know enough training to know that I wouldn't go about the job the way you propose to do it. Courses, methods, subject matter—all that comes last, if it comes at all. You have told me two important things. First, your hospital is extraordinarily complex—all these groups with different jobs, different backgrounds, and different needs. Secondly, you have at least three distinct areas in which people need to learn. They need to improve their technical skills on the job. They need to learn how to work with one another—nurses with x-ray people and dieticians, for instance. And they need to work on their skills and attitudes in caring for patients. Finally you have told me that there is one big group for which you need not and should not do much in-house training— your clerical and business people. What they need, particularly in respect to job skills, is amply provided for through evening courses, seminars and so on by colleges and by all kinds of management and professional societies. Your business manager should be expected to be your training director for clerical and business-office employees.

"But for the rest—and I gather that is three quarters of your employment or more—I would suggest that you pick some one who sees the job as being a trainer of trainers and a training coordinator rather than as that of a training *director*. I imagine it will be a nurse. Nurses apparently are the only people in the hospital who see and know the entire hospital rather than just their own segment, and who are in daily working relationship with all the other groups as well as with patients and doctors. Tell your candidate to spend ninety days sitting down with small groups from each area, the department head, say, and a handful of employees, both a few experienced ones and a few young and green ones. Tell her to ask these groups where they see *their* learning needs. Where do they see opportunities to do the job better? What do they have to know, what do they have to learn? What information and knowledge do they need and what tools? Make sure that they think through each of the three dimensions of the hospital job separately—technical skills, organizational relationships within the hospital and between its groups, and patient care. And then ask your new training director to submit to you a statement of learning priorities for each area and each group—and then you, the training director, and the department heads together work out a plan for in-hospital training. Then you'll find out what courses you need, where you want discussion groups, in what areas you are going to have each group have its own program—that'll probably be the case for most technical-skill areas, I imagine—and where you better bring people from various departments and areas together to learn from each other. Above all, emphasize to your training director and to your department heads that the training director's first job is not to be a trainer herself. It is to get other people to be trainers—nobody learns half as much as the person who is forced to teach. And what you are after isn't a big program and spending a lot of money. What you want is to create a climate of continuous learning throughout the whole hospital."

The hospital administrator was not impressed. "That's just common sense," he thought, "and one doesn't need to consult a big expert for *that*." But what do you think of the advice? Is it sensible? Is it realistic—the new training director, after all, is likely to be a novice at training no matter how good a nurse she might be.

And, assuming that the hospital administrator followed the advice, what kinds of things is the new training director likely to include in her priority list three months or six months hence?

Case Number 4

Are You One of "Us" or One of "Them"?

Labor relations at McDougal Machine Tools were considered exceptionally good by management as well as by the strong union. But socially "labor" and "management" kept apart from each other. Many of the workers were highly-skilled craftsmen, and many made a good deal more money than first-line foremen in the assembly plant or even the younger engineers and accountants. But no worker had, within living memory, been promoted out of the rank and file into a supervisory job, let alone into higher management. All supervisory jobs were staffed with engineering school graduates who were given a year's training under one of the plant superintendents and then served for another year or two as assistant foremen before being appointed foremen or staff engineers. Indeed the two groups lived in different parts of town. And only at such occasions as the annual Christmas Party did their families ever meet—and then they didn't mix. There was no hostility—on the job workers and supervisors used first names, joked together, helped each other, and clearly respected each other. But the two groups talked of each other as "us" and "them"—and because supervisory jobs tended to require substantial formal engineering knowledge both groups, apparently, thought this relationship appropriate—the natural order of things.

Gregory Armitage, who had come into the plant as a young assembly-line worker and had then worked his way up to highly skilled tool setter, had no quarrel with the system—indeed it made sense to him. But he was also an ambitious young man deeply interested in engineering. When, therefore, the local branch of the state university started an evening program in engineering, Gregory was one of the first to enroll. As it turned out, one of the plant's superintendents taught a course at the univerity and ran into Gregory at one of the first sessions. He beamed when he recognized one of his own workers, and from then on he did everything to help Gregory continue with his studies. It was he, for instance, who made sure that Gregory would not be given overtime assignments on evenings when his classes met. And he also made sure that Gregory got full tuition refund from the company even though the tuition-refund plan, strictly speaking, applied to salaried personnel only.

When Gregory finally got his degree he therefore called on the Superintendent who warmly congratulated him. But then Gregory said, "Now that I have an engineering degree, how do I apply for promotion to a foremanship? I believe I am fully qualified."

"You are indeed," said the Superintendent, "and yet I don't think it can work and I can't recommend you. We in management would welcome you. But I doubt that the men will accept you. You are one of them, and one of the younger ones to boot. They aren't going to accept you as one of us—not even if you move yourself and your family to the other side of town as you surely plan to do. The men will always wonder whether you are one of "us" or one of "them." They'll resent you if you exercise a foreman's authority, and they'll have no respect for you if you don't. I hate to say it, but I think you should try to get the supervisor's job you have earned someplace else where you can start fresh—I'll gladly help you get it."

Gregory accepted the offer—he had little choice, after all. He soon found himself working as supervisor for another company, where he did well and became plant superintendent within a few years. But he also found that the superintendent had been right in predicting that he would have to move with his family. After a few months his wife complained that she had no friends left in the old neighborhood. And he himself gradually drifted away from the many friends he had had among McDougal workers.

This is an American story. What makes it American is that in most other countries a Gregory Armitage could never have become supervisor or a member of management once he had started as a blue-collar worker. In other than blue-collar employment the line between "them" and "us" in this country is quite a bit less pronounced than in the plant, but in most other countries it is equally sharp in the office or in the retail store.

Is such a line a good thing to have in a plant—or in a society? Could a management do anything to eliminate it in its own plants, or at least to make it a little less rigid?

Case Number 5

Midwest Metals
and the Labor Union

In the mid-1960s, long before the mounting concern with health care and its cost explosion, Gene Kowalski, the President of the Union Local that represented most of Midwest Metals hourly-rated workers, called on the company's Industrial Relations Vice President, Frank Snyder. "Our members," said Kowalski, "are increasingly unhappy with the medical and hospital care they receive under the company's plan. They feel that it is second-class care— and I have checked their complaints and agree with them. You'd better do something about it." "Gene," said the industrial-relations V.P., "this is quite a coincidence. I have heard similar complaints from the supervisors and from our whole management group. At the same time that patient care under the plan is going down, costs are going up very fast; I have been pushed by top management to do something before they get out of control. And so, a few weeks ago, I asked our medical director, Dr. Furness, to look into the whole matter. Her report came in yesterday, and I was just going to call you to come over to discuss it with you. Dr. Furness thinks we ought to switch to a pre-paid clinic plan, similar to what Kaiser is doing in California and Health Insurance Plan (HIP) is doing in New York. It's a plan with salaried doctors in a clinic and perhaps with its own hospital, where one pays a fixed amount per person covered by the plan rather than pay for services after they have been performed. Helen Furness recommends that we appoint a task force to study how best to do this, and what the advantages and disadvantages were."

Kowalski was enthusiastic. He had been about to propose a similar approach. But he refused to take the chairmanship of the task force that was offered to him. "Under our contract, health care insurance is a management responsibility, and I can't participate in formulating a management plan." But he stayed close to the work of the task force. And he was in full agreement with its final recommendation to start a Midwest Medical Foundation that would have three cinics in the city, each staffed with twelve to fifteen salaried doctors, and owning its own small hospital—perhaps Park Street Hospital, which had an excellent plant but was in severe financial difficulties and probably available for a moderate amount. Midwest's 10,000 employees and their families would be barely enough to make such a plan work. But Dr. Furness, having checked with some of her colleagues in the city's other industries, felt confident that other major employers would soon join up too. The medical and hospital care offered by the new plan would be more comprehensive and better than the existing contract provided; yet, after a year or two there would probably be a substantial cost saving—as much as 40%. Still—on this Snyder was adamant—the company would continue to put aside the same amount of money as under the old plan. Any cost saving would go into a special fund for five years. Then it would be decided jointly by company and union whether the available savings should be used to improve the health-care plan (Snyder thought of including dental care or at least part of it), or for other employee benefits.

Kowalski was sure the plan would be welcomed by his members. "But, you know," he said to Snyder, "I can't accept a change in the contract; the executive committee of the local has to approve it and then submit it to the members for a vote. I don't foresee any trouble, though." He was wrong. When he presented the new plan to his executive committee, he was subjected to sharp questioning. "Does the new plan cost the company more or does it cost the company less?" was the persistent question. "It does cost less," said Kowalski, "but we'll get the savings anyhow." "Never mind who gets the savings," said his oldest and most respected executive-committee member. "What matters is that the company gains. And you can't convince me or anyone in the plant that it's a benefit to us if it costs the company less. We all know that the more it costs the company the better for us, and the less it costs the company the worse for us." And so the plan was voted down unanimously by the executive committee. This was in the mid-1960s. By now health-care costs have, of course, increased manyfold—but prepaid plans such as Dr. Furness proposed have at the same time lost much of their luster. And the union today would probably be willing to be a party to a task-force study, might even insist on it. The basic situation has not changed, however. Union members—and union leaders—do believe that the measurement of an employee benefit is not how much the workers benefit but how much it costs the company. And there are quite a few management people who agree with them, believing that costs rather than the benefits the costs produce are the measurement of employee benefits. What might explain this prevailing misconception? And what could be done to dispel it and to make possible a rational cost-benefit approach to employee benefits?

Case Number 6

Safety at
Kajak Airbase

At the end of his first staff meeting, the new commandant of Kajak Tactical Airbase asked two of his officers to stay behind—his Chief of Operations and his Chief Safety Inspector. "I know," he said, "that Kajak has the best safety record in Tactical Air Command. But I am not satisfied. I aim to run a base on which there are zero accidents." "Sir," said the Chief of Operations, "we try—but fighter airplanes are inherently dangerous." "They should be dangerous to the enemy," snapped the Commandant, "not to our men." "We have three approaches," said the Chief Safety Inspector, "and we might intensify all three of them. We study the equipment; of course, we have no control over design and manufacturing but when we find something that might cause an accident—or find that something has caused one—we make sure that it is re-designed. We train and we train and we train. And when there is any mishap, even one that doesn't injure anyone, we have a thorough inquiry and, if necessary, change the method of operations or the equipment and, of course, recommend appropriate punishment if the mishap is the result of sloppy or careless operations. We can intensify our work—I, for one, have always asked for more training time—but I doubt that we'll get a great deal out of more intensive efforts. This is already the most safety-conscious base I know." The Commandant was not impressed, however, and asked both men to come up with specific proposals—and he repeated his intention to run a base with zero accidents. After a week, the two officers reported. "I'd suggest a permanent safety competition," said the Chief of Operations, "as one approach. Post on the bulletin boards the names of the units that have no accidents in a month; recognize their performance; reward them—a few extra passes often do wonders; and make it clear that recommendation or promotion goes to officers and NCOs who stand out in the safety competition. At the

61

same time," continued the Chief of Operations, "we might borrow from industry. I have a few friends at General Motors who tell me that they run plants with zero accidents by relieving from responsibility pending investigation any supervisor who has even the slightest accident even if there is no injury; and they also relieve his boss until the inquiry is concluded. If the supervisor has a second accident within a twelve-months period, they remove him and demote his boss. The only excuse is equipment failure over which the supervisor had no control." "Not bad," said the Commandant, "although I'd have to go upstairs to get authority to remove or demote people—but perhaps there is some other way to accomplish the same end."

"Sir," said the Chief Safety Inspector, "I am impressed by my colleague's ideas and think we might try them. But I have three other proposals. One, we might systematically encourage accident-anticipation reports. We have a suggestion system that includes suggestions on safe operations—and it works well. But we might ask each commander and each supervisor to give us a monthly report on everything within his authority that might pose even the slightest potential safety hazard—whether equipment, operations, or the way we staff or train. My second possible suggestion would be for regular monthly safety meetings in each area of the base devoted to the question: what can each of us do to make the work totally safe? And—my third suggestion—we might have one presentation at each of these meetings in which one commander or supervisor reports on what methods he has found effective in making his operation accident-proof."

"Do you think you could do these things without running up costs to the point where we get Washington on our back, and without impairing the combat effectiveness of the Command?" asked the Commandant. Both men thought it could be done—or at least there was enough probability to try each approach experimentally in a part of the base. What do you think of these five proposals? What principles in managing people does each represent? How likely is each to have impact? Which are likely to be welcomed by the personnel on the base? Are any likely to be resisted? What does each assume about the causes of accidents?

Case Number 7

How Does One Analyze
and Organize Knowledge Work?

If she had had a jump-rope, Susan Binkley would have skipped down the whole length of New York's Park Avenue, and in broad daylight. As it was, she pirouetted at every red light. And she did something she hadn't done since she was in junior high school: she sang out loud, anything she could remember: snatches from musicals, folksongs, nursery rhymes. Some passers-by stared, others smiled as they saw a pretty young woman so obviously happy. And one old gentleman sagely remarked to another: "That girl must be very much in love."

But it wasn't love that made Susan dance down Park Avenue; it was success. And she was not a junior-high school kid but 29 years old, terribly serious, and a liberated career woman. Only an hour earlier, the Senior Vice President and second in command in the Corporate Banking Division of Citizens National Bank had called her into his office and said, "I'd like to be the first to congratulate you. The Executive Committee promoted you this morning to Banking Officer in the Corporate Division—less than three years after you joined as a trainee and faster than anyone has made it in all my fourteen years with the Bank. And I have more good news. I know that you want your own command. And I remember that you liked the three months you spent in our Houston office. Well, Bill Harris, who heads Houston, called up a few days ago and specifically asked when you'd be available to come down as his assistant manager. And so we want you to go down as soon as you can. Bill is going on vacation in seven weeks and wants you to come early enough so that he can show you the ropes—you'll be acting manager while he is gone. And by the end of the year we plan to bring Bill back to New York to take over a new petroleum and chemical-industry division. If you work out—and, Susan, I know you will, and so does Harris—you'll take over as his replacement. That's an assistant V.P. job and a full V.P. title within a year."

Well, thought Susan, I can be in Houston in two days. In fact, this saves a lot of arguments with Tommy and gives me a good reason to end this relationship without tears or scenes. But isn't it wonderful—Susan Binkley, Corporate Banking Officer; Susan Binkley, Assistant V.P.; Susan Binkley, Vice President—well she'd make it and be the first Chairwoman of the Board of a major Clearing House Bank!

Nothing had been further from Susan's mind when she graduated from college at age 22 than a career in banking. She had studied art and had intended to become a commercial artist. She had not been unsuccessful, had indeed been able to support herself—well, almost—for a few years. But she had gotten awfully tired of knocking at the doors of advertising agencies for work, had gotten even more tired of drawing bras and panties for department-store ads, and had gotten most tired of a diet of peanut-butter sandwiches which were usually all she could afford. It was sheer accident that she heard of the Citizens National Bank looking for trainees—and for women trainees to avoid being sued for discrimination against women. The personnel officer who interviewed her was rather skeptical of her commercial-art background but brightened when Susan mentioned a couple of computer courses she had taken in college and liked—and the Bank had given orders to *hire women*! And so Susan, at age 26, started as a management trainee and started at the same time to go to business school in the evenings to get her MBA; the personnel person had insisted on it as a condition of employment. To her immense astonishment Susan found that she liked bank work—or at least most of it, for the three weeks in Letters of Credit were not much fun. And she, who had always disliked school, found that she loved the business courses, especially accounting and management. Indeed she managed to get an A even in Statistics and so she had graduated—only three weeks earlier—at the head of her class and had actually given the valedictorian's speech at the school's commencement. And now she was going to run the Houston office.

Bill Harris was O.K. but she didn't think him a ball of fire. He *was* a well-trained banker, and she had learned more credit analysis from him than from anybody else in the bank. But he still thought clients should come, hat in hand, and beg for loans. What the Houston office needed was aggressive marketing. She had said that to the Senior V.P. when she came back, had thought then that it was a mistake, but realized now that he must have agreed with her—or else he wouldn't send her to Houston. That story about Bill Harris asking for her—Bill, after three months, had still not accepted that a woman could be a banker even though he was quiet about it after a few pointed remarks on her part.

Houston could easily do double the business. The customers were there and the bank had the right services at the right price. But the office needed to be organized; Bill Harris was just managing from day to day. Fortunately she had picked that topic for her big term paper in the management class (the prof had given her an "A" plus). The title was "POIM in the banking office," and POIM stood, of course, for PLANNING, ORGANIZING, INTEGRATING AND MEASURING. So she had a starting point—and by the time Harris had gone on his vacation she would have learned enough about the Houston office to convert this paper into an action plan. But the management prof had said something else as well: "After you have done the planning and organizing of the unit or business, you had better analyze and organize the work of individuals—and especially the work of knowledge workers. Work is done by people, not by units or companies. And knowledge work requires systematic analysis and organization even more than manual work, where we usually know what the end product should be. Knowledge work," the prof had said, "is the most important area for the application of scientific management."

"Well," said Susan, "I should begin with my own work as manager of the unit. What are the pieces? How can I improve each? What information and what tools do I need? How do the pieces fit together? After I've analyzed my own job, I'll take the two most important jobs we have—marketing loans and analyzing loan applications, and do the same with them. But it isn't time and motion study I need. I need a critical analysis of all major steps in the work."

Do you think Susan is right in her approach to knowledge work? And how might one go about finding the key pieces in such work?

SOCIAL IMPACTS AND SOCIAL RESPONSIBILITIES

PART FOUR

Case Number 1

The Peerless Starch Company
of Blair, Indiana

As long as anyone in Blair, Indiana, could remember, the Peerless Starch plant had always been the biggest thing in town. Built on a slight hill above the sluggish river, and designed to look as much like the Tower of London as anything in Indiana can, the plant dominated the town spiritually even more than it did physically.

Peerless was the largest employer in town, employing well over 8000 men out of a population of 120,000—or every fourth head of a family. It paid the highest wages, if only because most of the men were rated as skilled workers or technicians. And alone of all the large businesses in Blair, it was locally managed; the Peerless top management sat on the fifth floor of the big mill itself, in the "New Building" that had been put up in 1924. And from the chief executive officer—the grandson of the founder—on down, all executives were Blair men who had started in the mill and worked their way up—and who more often than not were second- or third-generation Peerless employees.

Peerless had started in Blair during the Civil War when the founder had developed one of the first methods to extract starch from corn. Until the 1940s, Peerless had only one mill. But the company had prospered so much that three additional mills were built in rapid succession during the years after World War II—one in Illinois, one in Texas, and, the biggest yet, in Oregon, built in the late 1950s.

But while Peerless had flourished, the town of Blair had not. During World War II it had boomed. But then Blair had gradually drifted into being first a run-down and then a depressed area. One after the other of the town's factories had laid off people and then finally closed their doors. The Peerless Mill in Blair seemed to be the only exception to this general rule of slow decay and downhill drift. But appearances were deceptive. Actually the Peerless Mill in Blair was in dire straits and was kept going only by the success of the new mills in other states.

Blair's sales were about one-fifth of the entire Peerless Company. But the Blair Mill employed almost half of Peerless' hourly-rated labor force and three quarters of Peerless' managerial and professional people. Unlike the other mills, Blair did not make its own raw materials but got intermediates from outside suppliers or from the other mills. It should therefore have needed less labor per unit produced. Instead it needed up to four times as much.

There were reasons for Blair's high costs—or at least there were arguments to justify them. The mill itself was a towering structure built to withstand the Crusaders' Armies but ill-equipped for modern production. All newer Peerless mills, for instance, were single-story buildings, whereas Blair had five stories capped by twin towers. Nobody at Blair ever got fired; if a man couldn't do a job, the word from the head office was: "Find him another one." If a new process came in, the workers on the old one were quietly moved to plant maintenance—or, if they had any skills, were made supervisors, with the ludicrous result that there were whole departments with more supervisors than workers. Above all, Blair considered itself a "quality mill"; and that apparently meant that nothing could be produced in quantity. But the central problem of Blair—and the greatest drain in money—was precisely that Blair did not turn out quality products. Rejection rates at Blair ran almost twice as high as at the other mills. What the Blair quality-control inspectors accepted provoked angry complaints from the customers. Indeed, as every one knew, the sales people spent little time selling. They spent most of their time talking customers into not sending the stuff right back to Blair as faulty and unuseable—often by granting the complaining customer a nice rebate. It never appeared in the Blair accounts but was charged off to "miscellaneous customer service."

Things had been drifting from bad to worse—and no one in Blair expected that they would ever change. But then suddenly, in the spring of 1975, a number of things happened simultaneously.

(1) The founder's grandson, the "old man" who had run Peerless for thirty-five years, died. And it turned out that the founding family owned practically no stock at all. Thereupon the outside directors, who had not dared speak up while the "old man" was alive, refused to appoint his son-in-law or his nephew as his successor. Instead they picked an outsider to become president and chief executive officer: John Ludwig, who was not even a native of Blair, let alone a chemical engineer or a starch machinist. In fact Ludwig had been with Peerless less than four years—and had been imposed on the "old man" by some of the outside directors. Having started after the Korean War as an industrial psychologist, Ludwig had first taught, then worked for the Pentagon as a training specialist, then in Industrial Relations for Ford where he helped reorganize one of the major divisions and then had become general manager of one of the smaller Ford Motor divisions. He came to Peerless in 1967 as its first "professional manager"—at least the first one in Blair—and as Executive Assistant to the President. The "old man" had kept him busy on the affairs of the other plants so that he knew very little about Blair. Although he had several times thought of resigning what he felt was a futile and frustrating assignment, he now found himself in charge.

(2) Even before the "old man" died, things had turned critical at Peerless, and especially at Blair. The market suddenly became competitive. Synthetic starches and adhesives were flowing on the market out of the labs of the chemical companies and the oil com-

panies and the rubber companies—businesses that never before had been competing on the starch market. Peerless and a few other companies used to have the field all to themselves—and carefully refrained from hurting each other too badly. But the newcomers didn't know what every one in the industry knew: that you can't make the market bigger by lowering price or improving product performance; all you can do is spoil the market for everybody. Worse still, the success of the newcomers seemed to disprove these old "truths."

(3) The new mills in Illinois, Texas, and Oregon managed to hold their own—indeed Oregon did phenomenally well and managed to bring out a highly profitable new line of synthetics (without even telling the folks in Blair Central Research) that quickly became industry leaders. But Blair came close to collapse. With supply abundant, customers flatly refused to tolerate the Blair quality—or lack of quality—anymore. Despite all the efforts of the sales department, whole carloads of the stuff came back—often with a curt note: "Don't bother to call on us any more; we have contracted to buy our supply elsewhere." And Blair which for years had been barely breaking even, plunged into the red. By mid-1975 Blair was losing more money than the other three mills made, so that Peerless no longer showed any profit and, indeed, barely managed to earn the interest on its fixed debt. Blair, clearly, was bleeding Peerless white.

As soon as Ludwig had become President, he asked the ablest man in Blair management—an Assistant Superintendent of the Blair Plant—to study what could be done with Blair. The result was a recommendation to spend some $25 million on modernizing the Blair plant. For this sum, the Assistant Superintendent promised, Peerless would get as modern a plant as any in the country (to build it from scratch would cost around $60 million). Employment in the modernized plant would shrink from 8000 to 2600.

Ludwig had resolved not to take any action until the Assistant Superintendent completed his study. But he wasn't idle during that time. He himself carefully studied the economics of Peerless, previously kept rather secret. It soon became apparent to Ludwig that economically and financially Blair was untenable. The only economically justifiable course was to close the Blair mill and not replace it. The existing mills in Illinois, Texas, and Oregon could easily replace Blair's production volume—at a fraction of Blair's cost and at superior quality. Closing Blair would entail very heavy short-run costs, mainly severance pay. But within six months the Peerless Company would have absorbed the loss and would have become profitable again. If Blair were kept going, no matter how successfully modernized, Peerless could at best hope to break even—and the capital required to rebuild Blair would use up all the credit Peerless could possibly command—if indeed that much money could be raised in Peerless' shaky condition.

Ludwig was deeply disturbed by this conclusion. He knew how much the Peerless Mill meant to Blair; without it there weren't going to be any jobs in the town. He himself was old enough to remember the Depression days when his father, a machinist in a Milwaukee automobile plant had been unemployed for three bitter years. Yet Ludwig also knew that he had to make a decision fast. When he was made President, he had asked the Board to give him six months to study the situation—and the Board had given him that much time only grudgingly. At that the Board had not really known how bad things were—and at the next Board meeting, in January 1976, he would have to tell them that the first nine months of 1975 had been catastrophic months. Surely at that meeting, if not before, the Board would expect him to have a definite recommendation.

As a business decision there was clearly no choice: Blair had to be closed. But what about the company's social responsibility to Blair and to the people who depended on the Peerless mill for their livelihood? The more Ludwig thought about this the more did he become convinced that Peerless had the social responsibility to try to save the Blair mill and the town with it. There was a fair chance, after all, that the rescue operation would succeed. He was not at all sure that his Board would go along—indeed he half-suspected that the Board would ask for his resignation rather than authorize spending $25 million on Blair. Still he saw no choice in conscience but to try. But before recommending to the Board that the Blair mill be remodelled, Ludwig thought it prudent to discuss the matter with an old acquaintance, Glen Baxter. Baxter had attended the same college as Ludwig, had wanted to become a minister and had actually had a year or two of divinity school, but had then turned to economics and was now the economist for the very union that represented the Peerless workers. Ludwig was really more interested in getting Baxter's support than in getting his advice—privately he had always considered Baxter somewhat of a "radical" and an "oddball." But Ludwig knew that he needed union support for any plan to rebuild Blair—and that his Board would not even listen to such a plan unless he could give assurances of union support. And surely Baxter would support a plan that maintained 2600 jobs for his members!

Much to Ludwig's surprise, Baxter did no such thing. On the contrary, he became almost violent in his opposition. "To invest all this money in rebuilding Blair," he said, "is not only financially folly; it's totally irresponsible, socially. You aren't just President of the Blair mill; you are president of the Peerless Company with its 8000 employees outside of Blair. And you propose to sacrifice the 8000 people you employ outside of Blair to the people at Blair. You have no right to do so. Even if you succeed and Blair survives, Peerless will have lost the capacity both to pay severance pay and pensions should you have to lay off more people, and to raise the money to modernize and expand the other mills and to maintain the jobs there. All right, John Ludwig, maybe you'll be a hero in Blair with your plan; maybe people there will think you've done great things for them. But in my book you'll be a cheap demagogue—as president of the company you are paid for doing the right thing and not for being popular."

"Of course," Baxter said, "we in the union will do everything to make closing Blair as expensive as possible for Peerless—we do have a responsibility towards our members. But for you to jeopardize the jobs and livelihoods of the workers in the healthy plants just because you have a guilty conscience about Blair's mismanagement all these years—that's the height of social irresponsibility."

Does Baxter have a case?

Case Number 2

The Bishop and the
Exodus from New York City

On Easter Sunday, 1976, the Episcopal Bishop of New York City, the Very Reverend Paul Moore, Jr., used his Easter Sermon in the Cathedral of St. John the Divine to attack businesses that were leaving New York City for the suburbs. "Managements have a social and moral responsibility to stay in the city and to maintain employment opportunities for the underprivileged, the blacks, and the Puerto Ricans. It is anti-social and incompatible with the duties of a Christian to prefer the admittedly great attractions of the suburbs and thus directly to increase the crisis of the city and the misery of those that cannot leave." Since this sermon was delivered at the height of New York City's fiscal crisis, it made a considerable stir, got on all the front pages, and was warmly applauded by New York City politicians, bankers and leaders. But it is doubtful that even the Bishop expected the sermon to have much impact; and after a few days it was, of course, forgotten.

But it did have a great impact on one man: Albert Theroux. Theroux, a born and bred New Yorker of the fifth generation and a life-long Episcopalian, had decided only a few weeks earlier to move his company out of New York City and into suburban Westchester County close to the Connecticut border. He had been fighting this move for a good many years even though his partners and his employees had been for it all along. It was not only that Theroux had no intention of moving out of New York City himself. He could hardly imagine living anyplace else; and he hated commuting and knew that at his age—he was nearing sixty—it would become increasingly burdensome. Mrs. Theroux—his second wife, whom he had married after his first wife had died—was a Municipal Court Judge in a New York City court and surely would have to maintain her residence within the city limits. Also the firm of Theroux, Bluestone & Ross—founded by Albert Theroux when he returned from World War II as a young officer and built by him into one of the world's foremost consulting engineering firms with more than 2000 employees—had only in 1966 moved into magnificent offices at the very tip of Manhattan. Theroux had designed the offices and loved them especially on clear days, when the view from the Theroux floors of the building encompassed the entire New York Bay from Sandy Hook to the George Washington Bridge and the Triborough Bridge. The best part of the view was the Verrazano Narrows Bridge; for which Albert Theroux personally had done most of the design-engineering; which he considered both his masterpiece and the most beautiful thing in the world; and which he loved more than he loved any of his three children.

Yet Theroux had slowly been forced into accepting the need to move out of his beloved office and out of New York City altogether. Otherwise it became increasingly clear, he wouldn't have much of a firm left. His clients were moving out—the Theroux professionals now spent more of their time driving to the clients' offices in the suburbs than they spent in their own offices at their drawing boards. It had become difficult to recruit new employees— engineers, secretaries, accountants, and receptionists. The work of the firm often demanded late hours—and increasingly employees refused to stay behind after 5 p.m., even though the firm provided a guard service and taxis to take them home. Three of his oldest and closest associates (one of them the partner whom Theroux had groomed to take over as his successor) left in 1973 and set up in practice for themselves in Fairfax, Connecticut. They soon managed to get the lucrative General Electric account, which Theroux had spent years developing. When asked why they had left, the three said—"Only one reason: New York City. You move out to the suburbs and we'll rejoin you like a shot."

Still Theroux resisted. But then, only a few months before Bishop Moore's Easter Sermon, two women employees who had worked late were forced at gun point into a car as they left the building, and then robbed, raped, and beaten by two masked men. One of the women, Theroux' senior cost estimator, was still in the hospital and would probably never be able to walk again without a cane. She had been Theroux second employee and the first black woman hired by an engineering firm in any capacity except as a cleaning woman. Although she had no more than a high-school education, she had become one of the firm's most effective professionals. When Theroux visited her in the hospital, she pleaded tearfully with him to move the firm's headquarters out of the city. "We have no right to expose the other women to what I've been through," she said. "We have a responsibility to protect them." Indeed it became clear soon that even the most loyal members of the firm would look for other jobs unless the headquarters were moved. And so, only two weeks before Theroux sat in his pew at St. John the Divine and listened to the Bishop denouncing managements who moved their firms out of New York City, Theroux had announced at a meeting of the firm's professional staff that the firm had acquired five acres near the New York-Connecticut border, had already engaged a well-known architectural firm and was planning to move out of the city in early 1978.

What the Bishop said deeply disturbed Theroux. And he felt it his duty to bring the matter up once more with his associates and to reconsider the firm's decision. But when he arrived at his office on Monday morning he found his secretary in tears. "Oh, Mr. Theroux," she wailed, "we are all so worried you'll change your mind about moving out of here. I don't want to leave the firm; I love working with you. But I had to promise my husband yesterday that I'll quit if we don't move out as soon as possible. He says he isn't going to keep on worrying himself sick over me every time I work late." And then, before lunch, Theroux was visited by the "engineers executive committee", a group of twelve, all highly respected, who served as the elected managing board for the professional semi-union of Thoroux engineers and draftsmen. "We've come to tell you that none of our members are going to stay with the firm if you change your mind about moving out. We've all had enough of commuting in dirty, broken-down trains that are never on time—yet our families won't live in the city and it's no place for women and children. We are afraid of being mugged every time we stay overtime, and yet we are professional people and feel a responsibility for the job and for meeting our deadlines. And we cannot afford any longer to pay confiscatory New York State and New York City taxes—nor can the firm afford to pay us more than competition pays so that we can make a living despite the taxes here. We have taken a quick poll this morning among the firm's people. And the secretaries and receptionists feel even more strongly that they want to get out—after all women are particularly endangered in the jungle New York City has become—and black women even more so than white ones. We hate to do this to you. But we know that we can find jobs; in fact we know that we can form our own consulting firm and have enough business within six months, to survive." And, one of the senior men in the group—the most highly respected design engineer—said, "Don't say 'Let's make another study': we need firm and irrevocable assurances right now, today—or we will be forced to start looking for other jobs."

"But," stammered Theroux, "what about the social responsibility Bishop Moore talked about, our social responsibility to the poor of the city, to the blacks and the Puerto Ricans? Don't we owe them something?" "Al," said the same senior design engineer, "I won't argue theology with a bishop—I am an atheist anyhow. But it seems to me that the Bishop forgot something: your responsibility as a manager is to your own people in your own company. Maybe as a leading businessman in the city you do have a responsibility for the city—though I doubt that our staying here is going to help anyone. But that, it seems to me, is at best a responsibility at one remove—are you responsible for something over which you have no control and no authority? The responsibility as managers to our own people, their family, their safety, their peace of mind—isn't that our first, our direct, our inescapable duty? And what good would it do the city anyhow if you decided to stay here? You wouldn't have any firm left to give employment and to pay taxes.

Case Number 3

"I Am Paid to Look After the Selfish Interests of the Coal Miners"

In the darkest days of World War II, when American soldiers were fighting bloody battles in the South Pacific and in North Africa while American war production was still way behind, John L.

Lewis, the head of the United Mine Workers Union and then the most powerful labor leader in America, called his men out on strike against a refusal of the Government's War Labor Board to raise coal miners' wages above the wage limits set by the Government. Coal in those days was even more central to the American economy than it is now. All railroads ran on coal, it heated most homes, all electric power stations were fueled by it, and it was the primary raw material of steel making. A coal strike of even short duration meant a sharp setback in war production; a long coal strike would have brought the whole economy to a complete stop. There was thus universal outcry when Lewis called a coal strike—even within the labor movement. But Lewis didn't budge. Finally President Roosevelt publicly assailed Lewis for "putting the selfish interests of the coal miners above the national survival of the United States." And Lewis retorted: "You, Mr. President, are paid to take care of the survival of the United States. I am paid to take care of the selfish interests of the coal miners"—and he did not call off the strike until most of his demands had been met.

No one today would dare say what Lewis said twenty-five years ago—and few would even think it. But is there nothing to be said for Lewis' position?

Case Number 4

Civil Rights and the Quaker Conscience

In the late 1940s, a major American steel company appointed a new general manager for its large southern division, located in one of the most strongly "white supremacy" areas in the South. Traditionally, all top-management positions in that division had been held by Southerners. The new appointee was a Northerner. Moreover, he was a member of one of the old Philadelphia Quaker families and had been active in several civil rights organizations.

Upon his appointment, top management called him in and said, "We know what we are doing and why we are appointing you. To be sure, your performance has earned you this promotion. But you are also a Northerner and committed to employment equality for blacks. And this, of course, is what both the laws of the United States and our union contract demand of us. Yet, as we all know, our southern division has never given equal employment opportunities to blacks. No black, however skilled, no matter what his job, has ever been paid more than helper's wages. But we know that we will not be able much longer to defend and to keep up these practices. We expect you, therefore, to move as fast as you can for civil rights for our Negro employees, as the laws of the country and our union contract demand. Try to get the support and cooperation of the top people in the union that represents our workers. We know that you have been working with them in several civil rights organizations."

The new general manager spent a year quietly establishing himself in the company, getting known in the local community, and establishing friendly relations with the union leaders in the mill. Then he saw his opportunity. A new major extension to the mill was about to be opened, and a number of new furnaces had to be manned. The new general manager strictly applied the hiring provisions of the union contract. As a result, a small but still substantial number of black workers with high job skills and considerable seniority got positions on the new crews. In no case was a white worker deprived of his seniority rights or put under a black man as his supervisor.

The morning after the new positions had been posted, as required by the union contract, a delegation of local union leaders called on the general manager. "You know that there are several hundred grievances," they said, "which have been pending for far too long a time without a settlement. The patience of our men is exhausted. We are going out on strike in thirty-six hours. But we don't want to be unreasonable. If the company makes even a token gesture of goodwill, we will postpone this strike. All you have to do is to suspend those new assignments you just posted, and let us, together with the supervisors, work out the composition of the crews for the new furnaces. In the meantime, here is the official strike notice as required by our contract."

The general manager first tried to reach the president and the general counsel of the union. Unaccountably, neither could be found, nor did their secretaries know where they could be reached or when they would return. Then the general manager thought of an old friend, one of the "sages" of the Quakers and a "radical" on race relations, and especially on employment opportunities for blacks. But to the general manager's immense surprise, the "sage" was not one bit sympathetic with his plight. "I fully agree with you, as you know, in considering employment discrimination against the Negro to be illegal, immoral, and sinful," the sage said. "But what you have done, while legal, is just as immoral. You have used the economic muscle of a big company to impose your values on the community in which you operate. Yours are the right values. But, still, you are using the economic power of a business, the power of the employer, and the authority of your office to dictate to the community. This is 'economic imperialism' and it cannot be condoned, no matter how good the cause."

The general manager resigned and took another job up north. The company quietly dropped the proposed job assignments. The mills remained open. And a few years later, needless to say, the company came under bitter attack for its failure to take leadership in race matters. As the biggest employer in the community, the critics charged, the company had a social responsibility not to condone practices which it must have known to be both illegal and immoral. But would it have been compatible with a company's social responsibilities to enforce its belief on a Southern community earlier, when public opinion, labor unions, and community did not yet accept them?

Case Number 5

Bribery or

Patriotic Duty?

For almost three years Philip Kendrick, of the law firm of Boswell, Johnson & Kendrick had been working with the Kabata Machine Tool & Compressor Company of Osaka, Japan, to find the right location for a big American plant Kabata had decided to build—a plant designed eventually to employ 3500 people and to produce the full Kabata line for American customers as well as for export all over the world. Fairly early in the project the choices had narrowed down to sites near the Southeastern seaboard, especially to a handfull of deep-water ports between Wilmington, Delaware and Jacksonville, Florida. Several times it seemed that a decision had been reached. The plant with its promise of 3500 jobs was a prize plum for which cities competed aggressively. But at the last minute there was then always a hitch—some unresolved environmental-impact problem; some problem of zoning or of taxes and so on. Kendrick felt every time that the problem was minor and would take care of itself and advised his clients at Kabata to go through with the deal and tackle the problem later. But they demurred. "Unless we know we are completely welcome," the management people at Kabata said, "we aren't going to move. We don't want to be known as "ugly Japanese"—and we know that there'll be enough local prejudice against a Japanese company." The member of Kabata management who held this view most tenaciously was Shujiro Wakayama, the Senior Executive VP in charge of international business. Both because of his assignment and because he was the only member of Kabata top management who spoke good English—acquired as a youngster during the Occupation Period when he served as interpreter for an American Colonel who was military governor of his home town—Wakayama had been working closely with Kendrick. And while Kendrick deplored Wakayama's conservatism he had come to respect the man's basic integrity.

Finally Kabata had found the site it wanted—and the city and state were more than happy and worked out all details to Kabata's satisfaction. The only remaining problem—but a big one—were the conditions of the loan which Kabata needed. Kabata did not want a subsidy even though the State had offered one; indeed, Kabata was rather insulted when the offer was being made. But Kabata balked at the interest rate which the bank demanded and asked instead for a state guarantee for the loan which would, of course, have meant a much lower interest rate—2 full percentage points lower—and an annual interest saving of more than $3 million. This, however, the Governor of the State and his legal counsel were reluctant to give. They feared criticism from the companies already in the state, who had to do business without such help, and the State's Finance Director was totally opposed. He pointed out the adverse impact such a guarantee, no matter how well protected by pledges from the Kabata Company back in Japan, might have on the state's credit rating.

Kendrick was pretty sure that both sides were ready for a compromise. But he also realized that both sides had to do some hard bargaining before accepting a compromise. The Governor had to be able to convince his critics in the press and the legislature that he had gotten the best deal possible; and so did Wakayama in dealing with his colleagues and his Japanese bankers. Accordingly Kendrick set up a meeting in the Governor's office—with the Governor's legal counsel and the State Finance Director present in addition to the Governor himself—and asked Wakayama to come over from Osaka for the meeting. Wakayama agreed but stipulated that he would be accompanied by an interpreter—even though his English was probably more than adequate. "In Japan we wouldn't expect an American to appear without an interpreter no matter how well he speaks Japanese," he pointed out. "I have to be absolutely sure I understand what is being said; and the Governor and his associates have to be absolutely sure they know what I say." Fortunately Kendrick had the right person available, an interpreter who knew both the subject matter and Wakayama. She had been Wakayama's secretary and interpreter in his dealings with Kendrick, until she quite recently married one of Kendrick's associates in the firm and his assistant in the Kabata business. Michiko-san was delighted to work with her old associates again.

After introductions and polite preliminaries were over in the Governor's office, Wakayama asked to say something by way of opening the meeting. He then proceeded to say "Mr. Governor and you other gentlemen from the State Government, I realize that you have reason to wonder whether a Japanese firm knows how to behave in your country. So let me assure that we know what is required. We hope and expect that you, Mr. Governor, and you other gentlemen, will join the Board of our American subsidiary when you become available for such appointments—and of course we expect to pay adequate remuneration for such service. And I can assure you that I speak for all my colleagues."

Fortunately Wakayama said this in Japanese—and Michiko-san

was quick enough to realize that she should ask Kendrick's advice before translating. When she told him what Wakayama had said, Kendrick almost fainted. Fortunately none of the State offiicials understood a word of Japanese, so the meeting proceeded without translation of Wakayama's remarks. It came, as Kendrick had expected, to a compromise solution which both sides happily accepted.

When they were out of the Governor's office, Wakayama turned to Kendrick and said: "I am most surprised and really somewhat angry, Mr. Kendrick, that you told Michiko-san not to translate the very important words with which I opened the meeting. And I am at a complete loss why you did something that could only damage our relations with the Governor and his associates—you owe me an explanation."

Thereupon Kendrick exploded. "You darn fool," he almost shouted, "don't you realize that both of us would be in jail if I had let Michiko-san translate your clumsy attempt at bribery? At the very least, the Governor would have been forced to have both of us thrown out of his office immediately—and since there were witnesses to your brazen offer of a big bribe for giving you a state guarantee for your bank loan, the Governor would have had no choice but to call a press conference and denounce you and me—and I can assure you after that you wouldn't be able to build a plant anyplace in the United States and would surely lose most of your American customers. And personally I am not only deeply upset by your stupidity, I am also deeply insulted. I am sure you wouldn't have said these things to a Japanese government official."

Wakayama looked at him wide-eyed. "Bribery? Jail? I don't understand a word you're saying. Of course I wouldn't have said what I said in Japan—there would have been no need to. They know us there as decent people. They know we know our patriotic duty. They know we know that a major business is expected to take care of senior government officials when they leave office—how else can they make ends meet and how else can you get decent and able people to work in poorly-paid government jobs? In Japan I would long ago have sent a mutual friend to give my greetings to the Governor and to let him know that we in Kabata hope that our association will continue for years to come—and that's all I'd have to say at home. But I can't expect you in this country to know that we have a reputation we treasure, that we know our duty as citizens and businessmen and that we know how to behave—so it had to be said."

Kendrick knew Wakayama well enough to realise that he, Kendrick, had blundered—though he could not figure out how. He was so puzzled however that he sought out his old Professor of Comparative Government who, he remembered, was considered an expert on Japan. The old man chuckled when Kendrick told him the story. "Yes," he said, "in the U.S. that's clearly attempted bribery and a criminal offense. But everyplace else that's a patriotic duty. They do it a little differently in different countries. In Japan the senior civil servant who reaches the top rung of the ladder but doesn't get beyond it expects to be offered a juicy sinecure in business. In the first place that senior man is expected to leave government employment if he doesn't make it to the top—he was in the running, after all, and so he'd better not stay around if some one else gets the big promotion, gets to be Vice Minister for instance. And the Japanese do not believe it right to pay high salaries to public servants or to pay high pensions. So who then looks after that senior man who has made a major contribution and had a great career but never made much money and doesn't get too much of a pension—and who yet had better leave government service "for the good of the service"? It's clearly the patriotic duty of business to enable the public service to attract and hold good people and to enable the public service to function, and that means taking care of the senior man when he leaves government service. In France the same situation prevails. It is tacitly understood that top positions in big business are to be reserved for men who got to be top-ranking civil servants, are in the running for the sub-cabinet jobs but don't get them because they don't fit politically, and who then are expected to leave government service rather than be an embarrassment. You won't find any one else in the top ranks of major French companies except in a few ones that are still family-run. In Germany that fellow is expected to be offered a well-paid job as executive secretary of a trade association—a highly prestigious job in Germany and better paid than most senior executive jobs except in the very biggest companies. In England it used to be that such men were automatically put on boards of of companies with a substantial stipend. Indeed, the company or industry that fails to take care of these distinguished middle-aged civil servants (in every country other than the U.S.) is clearly considered to be remiss in its social responsibility. Business has a social responsibility to enable public service to attract good people and to function. Of course, we in this country, see it quite differently. When I was younger, I thought *we* were right—indeed I helped a good deal to tighten our Conflict-of-Interest laws for our civil servants. I am no longer sure this is right; maybe these other countries have a better idea. Surely they don't suffer any—there is no evidence of more corruption or more favoritism—and the senior civil servant can afford to be more concerned with the public good and less with his own future which, if he gets the reputation of being first-class, is likely to be underwritten by business." Concluded the professor, "We know it's bribery; the rest of the world is equally convinced it's the social responsibility of business. And I'd be hard pressed to say who is right."

Who is? Or can they both be right? Perhaps the difference lies less in concepts of social responsibility than in the different ways different countries perceive the relationship between government and business?

Case Number 6

Union Carbide and Vienna, West Virginia

West Virginia, never one of the more prosperous areas of the United States, went into rapid economic decline in the late twenties as the coal industry, long the state's mainstay, began to shrink. The decline of the coal industry was hastened by rising concern with mine accidents and miners' diseases. For many of the coal mines of West Virginia were small and marginal and could not afford modern safety precautions or adequate health protection.

By the late 1940s, the leading industrial company in the state became alarmed over the steady economic shrinkage of the region. Union Carbide, one of America's major chemical companies, had its headquarters in New York. But the original plants of the company had been based on West Virginia coal, and the company was still the largest employer in the state, together with a few large coal mining companies. Accordingly, the company's top management asked a group of young engineers and economists in its employ to prepare a plan for the creation of employment opportunities in West Virginia, and especially for the location of the company's new plant facilities in areas of major unemployment in the state. But for the worst afflicted area—the westernmost corner of the state on the border of Ohio—the planners could not come up with an attractive project. In and around the little town of Vienna, West Virginia, there was total unemployment, and no prospects for new industries. There was, however, also considerable unrest in the area, great bitterness, and a good deal of feeling against "big business" from "outside the state". Indeed, whenever a tax measure came up in the State Legislature, the representatives of the Vienna area asked for high taxes so business—and in a few instances they had blocked and defeated tax bills of considerable importance to Union Carbide's plants in other areas of the state.

Top management was keenly aware of the situation. The whole idea of a strategic plan for new plants in West Virginia had started with a question by the president, himself originally a miner's son from a small town not far from Vienna: "What can we do to help Vienna's economy and employment?" But the only thing the study would find as even a remote possibility for Vienna was a ferro-alloy plant using a process that had already become obsolete and had heavy cost disadvantages compared to more modern processes such as Union Carbide's competitors were using.

Even for the old process, Vienna was basically an uneconomical location. The process required very large amounts of coal of fair quality. But the only coal available within the area had such high sulfur content that it could not be used without expensive treatment and scrubbing. Even after this heavy capital investment, the process was inherently noisy and dirty, releasing large amounts of fly ash and noxious gases.

The only rail and road transportation facilities were not in West Virginia but across the river, on the Ohio side. Putting the plant there, however, meant that the prevailing winds would blow the soot from the smokestacks and the sulfur released by the power plants directly into the town of Vienna, on the other bank of the river.

Yet the Vienna plant would provide 1,500 jobs in Vienna itself and another 500 to 1,000 jobs in a new coal field not too far distant. In addition, the new coal field would be strip-mined, so the new jobs would be free from the accident and health hazards that had beome increasingly serious in the old worked-out coal mines of the area. Union Carbide top management came to the conclusion that social responsibility demanded building the new plant, despite its marginal economics.

The plant was built with the most up-to-date antipollution equipment known at the time. Whereas even big-city power stations were then content to trap half the fly ash escaping from their smokestacks, the Vienna plant installed scrubbers to catch 75 percent—though there was little anyone could do about the sulfur dioxide fumes emitted by the high-sulfur coal.

When the plant was opened in 1951, Union Carbide was the hero. Politicians, public figures, educators, all praised the company for its social responsibility. But ten years later the former savior was fast becoming the public enemy. As the nation became pollution-conscious, the citizens of Vienna began to complain more and more bitterly about the ash, the soot, and the fumes that floated across the river into their town and homes. In 1961 a new mayor was elected on the platform "fight pollution," which meant "fight Union Carbide." Ten years later the plant had become a "national scandal." Even Business Week—hardly a publication hostile to business—chastised Union Carbide (in February, 1971) in an article entitled "A Corporate Polluter Learns the Hard Way."

Yet this is not the basic less of this cautionary tale. Once the decision had been made to employ an obsolescent process and to build an economically marginal plant in order to alleviate unemployment in a bitterly depressed area, the rest followed more or less automatically. This decision meant that the plant did not generate the revenues needed to rebuild it. There is very little doubt that on economic reasoning alone the plant would never have been built. Public opinion forced Union Carbide to invest substantial sums in that plant to remedy the worst pollution problems—though it is questionable whether the technology exists to do more than a patch-up job. Publicity also forced Union Carbide to keep the plant open. But, once the spotlight shifts elsewhere, most of the jobs in the Vienna, West Virginia plant are likely to disappear again, if indeed the plant remains open at all. And there is still no other employer in the area.

Was it "socially responsible" to build the plant in the first place? Was it "socially responsible" to keep it running once changing concepts of the balance between pollution and jobs created an environmental problem? Would it have been "socially responsible" to pour additional millions in to clean up the plant when it could never hope to become a competitive producer? And would it be "socially responsible" for Union Carbide to close the plant?

Case Number 7

Deltec and Swift
Do Argentina

The Swift meat-packing plant in the Buenos Aires port district has been the largest meat-packing plant in Argentina for many years. It has also been a major employer in a poor area of Buenos Aires. Originally a subsidiary of Swift of Chicago, the company became independent, though still under American ownership, shortly after World War II.

But the Argentinian meat-packing industry fell on evil days after World War II—in part because of government measures that have been driving up the price of Argentinian cattle, while cutting down the supply, thus making Argentinian beef increasingly noncompetitive in the world market and depriving meat-packers of their source of raw materials. Swift became increasingly unprofitable. The owners finally sold out in 1968 to a Canadian-based "multinational," Deltec, a company that is active in many parts of Latin America, primarily in financial service businesses. Deltec promptly started to modernize the Swift plant to make it competitive again. But the Argentinian meat-packing industry continued on its decline.

Swift's two major competitors, both foreign-owned, decided in the late 1960s to close down. They paid off the workers according to Argentinian law and went out of business. Deltec, however, decided that it could not afford to do this in view of its many other interests in Latin America. It had to maintain employment in an area where unemployment was far too high anyway. Deltec worked out an agreement with the labor unions under which employment was substantially cut and productivity greatly improved. The company poured substantial amounts of money into the plant and used its financial connections to obtain foreign bank loans for it. Still the meat business in Argentina did not improve.

By 1971 Swift had used up all the capital Deltec could make availability to it and was still not back on a profitable and competitive basis. Thereupon Swift worked out a voluntary agreement with the creditors, including the company's workers, for full repayment of all debts over an extended period—with Deltec being the last creditor to receive any payment. Eighty-six percent of the creditors, far more than required by law, accepted this agreement. But to everyone's surprise the Argentinian judge, whose approval had been expected as a mere formality, turned the agreement down. He decided that Deltec had obtained it improperly, declared Swift do Argentina bankrupt, ordered its liquidation, and asked the Argentinian government to appoint a liquidator. In effect he expropriated the company and its property. He not only refused to recognize any rights of Deltec as a creditor but decided that all Deltec holdings in other Argentinian companies be impounded as security for Swift's debts to Argentinian creditors.

There was no public pressure for such an action—and no legal pressure either. The Swift workers, although members of the most militant of Argentinian unions, fully supported Deltec. Yet the decision found tremendous approval in Argentina, even among people who by no stretch of the imagination could be considered antibusiness or even anti-American. "The other foreign-owned meat-packers," a good many people said, "did the right thing in closing down their plants and paying off their workers when they could no longer operate economically. Deltec, by trying to keep going, raised expectations which it then cruelly had to disappoint."

THE MANAGER'S WORK AND JOB

PART FIVE

Alfred Sloan's
Management Style

Rarely has a chief executive of an American corporation been as respected and as revered as Alfred P. Sloan, Jr., was at General Motors during his long tenure at the top—from 1920 until 1955. Many GM managers, especially those who grew up in the twenties and thirties, felt a deep personal gratitude to him for his quiet but decisive acts of kindness, of help, of advice, or just of warm sympathy when they were in trouble. At the same time, however, Sloan kept aloof from the entire managerial group in GM. That he never called anyone by his first name and was Mr. Sloan even to top executives may have been a reflection of his generation and upbringing—he was born, after all, in the 1870s and was a senior executive, running his own business, before 1900. However, unlike most of his generation, he also addressed the black elevator men in the GM building in Detroit or New York in the same way. They were always Mr. Smith or Mr. Jones. When he met a new elevator attendant, he would introduce himself. "I am Mr. Sloan. What is your name?" When the man answered, "I am Jack, sir," Sloan would turn white with anger and would say, "I asked for your name, sir,"—and would from then on always remember it. Sloan also frowned on the use of first names by his top people among themselves. It was known, for instance, that he felt it unwise of Mr. Wilson—for many years GM's President and later Sloan's successor as Chief Executive Officer—that he was on first-name terms with most of GM's vice-presidents.

Above all, Sloan had no friends within the GM group. He was a warm and had been a gregarious man until deafness cut him off from easy human contact. Although he had had close friends, he outlived them all—he lived well into his nineties. All these friends had been outside General Motors. Indeed the one friend who had been in GM, Walter P. Chrysler, did not become a personal friend until after he had left GM and had, upon Sloan's advice and with strong support from Sloan, started his own competing automobile company.

As Sloan grew older, he felt keenly his increasing isolation as his close friends died one by one. Yet he remained aloof from GM people. He never invited them to his home. Unless it was a business meeting with a clear business agenda, he did not even sit down to a meal with any of them. He never accepted an invitation to any of their homes, even on business trips to their home towns. He was once asked how he liked Winterthur, the estate of Pierre DuPont who had been his boss at GM in 1919 and 20 and Chairman of the GM board for years thereafter. "I have never been to any of the Du-Pont homes," he answered. "Ours is a business relationship." In his earlier years Sloan had been a keen outdoorsman—but his hiking, fishing, and camping companions had all been non-GM people. Only after his retirement in 1955, when advancing old age made it more and more difficult for him to travel, did he invite GM people to come to his home in New York—and then only to discuss business in the office wing of his apartment—for he was still a GM Director and a member of the top committees.

"It is the duty of the Chief Executive Officer to be objective and impartial," Sloan said, explaining his management style. "He must be absolutely tolerant and pay no attention to how a man does his work, let alone whether he likes a man or not. The only criteria must be performance and character. And that is incompatible with friendship and social relations. A Chief Executive Officer who has 'friendships' within the company, has 'social relations' with colleagues or discusses anything with them except the job, cannot remain impartial—or at least, which is equally damaging, he will not appear as such. Loneliness, distance and formality may be contrary to his temperament—they have always been contrary to mine—but they are his duty."

What do you think of this? And would such successful Chief Executives as Abraham Lincoln or Franklin D. Roosevelt have agreed?

Case Number 2

Misdirection by Compensation: G.E.'s Experience

In the early 1950s the General Electric Company started on a massive reorganization. The company was decentralized into a large number of product businesses, each with its own responsibility for profit and loss performance. As part of this process executive compensation was restructured to give the general manager of each product business and his associates substantial participation in the profits of his unit. This was greeted enthusiastically by the managerial group in G.E. who had long complained that their salaries and bonuses had no relationship to company or business results.

The product businesses were also charged with responsibility for technical and product innovation in their assigned area. Top management hoped that this would greatly speed technological innovation and the development of new products. Instead technological and product innovation—the areas on which G.E. had always prided itself and on which its leadership position had been built—slowed to a crawl, and in many areas, stopped altogether.

No one could figure out, at first, what was happening. Indeed for a long time everybody in the company stoutly denied that it *was* happening. But gradually it became clear that the compensation system was largely to blame. It rewarded managers handsomely for return on capital. But as one veteran head of one of G.E.'s large businesses finally pointed out, this rewarded them for getting the most out of yesterday and today, but penalized them for putting any money or effort into the new, the different, the innovative. "Everything new," he pointed out, "for five years is only cost and no profit, only investment and no return. And my colleagues and I are being measured, judged, and rewarded on what profit we produce *this year*. All right, we can justify 'research' spending; but the big money is, of course, the money spent for development and market introduction. If we spend that, we cut down our profits and with them our own incomes. We also get severely criticized by the accounting and operations-research people in central office for building up 'unproductive overhead.' "

Do you think this is a common situation? What can be done to remedy it? And what can one learn from it in respect to the management of managers?

Case Number 3

Can You Manage
Your Boss?

After four years of working under Pete Webster, Larry Frankenmuth had had it. The work itself was fine—he was in charge of the company's four metal-working plants, knew the work, liked it, and was sure he did a good job. His subordinates were great. Every one of the four plant managers was first-rate, easy to work with, competent, on top of his job. The company was fine and clearly going places. The pay was good.

But *Webster!* Webster was a pain in every part of Larry's body from top to toe. Never an encouraging word, only grunts or criticism. Larry slaved on the memoranda and reports he sent up to Webster's office—and he never heard anything about them. He always made sure to be in Webster's office first thing in the morning with anything important—or to call him at 8:30 sharp. His first boss had drilled that into him when Larry started as a manufacturing engineer. Yet Webster always acted as if Larry had broken all ten commandments when he knocked at the door and asked whether he could come in. "'What have you to see me about *again*, Frankenmuth," he'd growl. But he'd also bite his head off if Larry did not tell him to the last detail any single thing that was going on, and especially any bad news ahead. But the worst thing about Webster was his appalling illiteracy. Larry Frankenmuth—with a B.A. and an M.A. in mechanical engineering from M.I.T.—had then, on his own time, gone and taken all the courses he could get in modern management, in modern production, in operations research and in quantitative methods. Then to have to work for a boss who hadn't finished high school! Webster had gone into the army in 1941 at the end of his junior year in high school and then started as a machinist when he came back from the service. He probably couldn't even do long division and surely could not follow the simplest regression analysis. It was too much!

And so Larry Frankenmuth decided to leave. He realized that he had made the decision on a Sunday evening when he had worked at home on a careful study of order patterns and production schedules, adding up to a recommendation to change production scheduling, inventory control, and shipping schedules for all four plants of the metal-working division. It was the most searching analysis he had yet made, and he felt very good about it. But as he was about to put the pages together for his secretary to type out the following morning, he suddenly realized that there was absolutely no point in showing the work to Webster. "The old coot just couldn't understand," he said to himself. "And if he could, he'd still be much too reactionary to make any change in what has been procedure since before I was born. He'll never even read the report, I bet. And instead of discussing the figures he'll treat me to one of his endless anecdotes about the good old days. I just can't take any more of it."

And so without even telling his wife, Lois, he set about finding another job. He had little difficulty in finding one. The new job was not quite as big, not quite as well paid, and with a company that had only limited growth opportunities, but the company was a highly technological one, and so Larry's management-science was fully appreciated. Indeed, Larry was now the one who felt somewhat under-educated, since so many of his new associates had Ph.D.'s. Lois approved; she had long known how frustrated Larry had been. Webster approved in his boorish fashion. When Larry went in to tell him, he only said: "I won't try ot talk you out of it. I have to tell you, Frankenmuth, that I could not and would not have recommended you for a promotion. Your leaving makes it much easier for all of us." And so Larry packed his papers and prepared to move out of the office in which he had suffered four long years.

Two days before he left, he had an unexpected visitor, Frank Sartorius, the plant manager who was to take Larry's job. Sartorius' selection had surprised Larry. Larry had been sure Webster would pick the oldest and most conventional of his four plant managers. Instead he chose the youngest—Sartorius was well under forty—the most innovative, the boldest. In fact Larry had to admit to himself that he would have hesitated to take the gamble. Sartorius had been plant manager only a few years, and Larry doubted whether he was really ready yet. Larry had gotten along fairly well with Sartorius, but did not consider himself close to the man. Larry was therefore somewhat surprised when Sartorius called up, said that he was coming to the headquarters city in a day or two and would like a private, off-the-record session at Larry's home. He was even more surprised when Sartorius said, "Larry, I was quite shocked when I heard that you were leaving. I was even more shocked when Webster called me and told me I'd take over from you. I didn't expect a big promotion for another three, four years, if then. What can you tell me that will help me?"

Larry spent an hour or two discussing the plants and their managers, and another hour talking about the relationships and problems inside the company—in particular about a long-standing feud with Purchasing and about the rather prickly personnel department and its failure to back operating management against the union. Finally he said, "Frank, I guess you know most of this," and Frank Sartorius nodded. "But," continued Larry, "the really important thing about this job isn't the plants, it isn't Purchasing or Personnel or the accountants. It is that impossible S.O.B., the boss. He doesn't read a line—you might as well write on water. He never has a word of praise, never, but is quick to criticize. He expects you to keep him informed about everything and is positively indecent in his insistence that you inform him ahead of time of anything unexpected. Yet he bites your head off when you come in to tell him. He is such an old reactionary that you just don't dare propose any change. You'll have no real trouble with any part of your job—it's in good shape, and the men are a pleasure to work with—but you just won't be able to manage the boss."

Larry Frankenmuth soon forgot all about his old company—the new job turned out to be a great deal tougher than he had expected and kept him fully occupied. He once ran into old Webster at the airport and asked him how Sartorius was doing—only to get a gruff "Why should I tell you?" for an answer. So he was quite surprised to read three years later, in the *Wall Street Journal*, that Frank Sartorius had been appointed to succeed Pete Webster as manufacturing vice-president when Webster moved up to executive vice president in charge of the metal-working and mechanical divisions. "I must send Sartorius a note of congratulations when I get home tonight," he said to himself. But when he got back home he found that Sartorius had anticipated him. On the hall table was a huge flower pot with a handwritten note from Sartorius:

> Dear Larry Frankenmuth,
> You will have heard that I have been promoted to VP—Manufacturing—and I owe it all to you and want to say "Thank You." You have taught me that I had to learn to manage the boss. And you told me how to do it.
> > Cordially,
>
> > Frank Sartorius

Can you tell the dumbfounded Larry Frankenmuth what Sartorius meant? And what did Larry tell Sartorius about managing that tough, reactionary S.O.B. of a boss, Pete Webster?

Case Number 4

Ross Abernathy and
the Frontier National Bank

The Frontier National Bank was the oldest bank in one of the country's rapidly growing regions. For many years it had also been the region's biggest and most profitable bank. But beginning around the time of World War II it had become increasingly stodgy—at Frontier they preferred to call it conservative—and had steadily lost market standing and, beginning around 1955, profitability. By the late seventies it had slipped to third place in assets in its region, and to sixth place in profits. It was still one of the nation's best known banks, and with about seven billion dollars in assets, still a very big bank. But it did mainly routine business with traditional customers. This it accomplished with an enormous staff—almost twice as many employees per dollar of assets as the number one bank in the region—and at a snail's pace.

In 1977 the bank was still headed by a member of the founding family—the founder's great grandson. The family no longer held any stock worth speaking of, but the bank still spoke reverently of the Family. So, when the head man reached age 70 and the bank's retirement age, he proposed, as a matter of course, that his son-in-law succeed him. To his—and everybody else's—surprise, the Board balked. Indeed during the preceding year, with the old man's retirement imminent, the Comptroller of the Currency (who supervises all national banks) had forced the Board's hand. He had conveyed to key members of the Board his concern over the rapidly falling profitability of the bank, its declining liquidity, and inadequate capital. And he had hinted broadly that he would not be at all opposed to a proposal to merge Frontier with one of its younger, more dynamic, and better-managed competitors.

The Board appointed a search committee which speedily agreed that they had to look at the outside for a new Chief Executive Officer. And they had little difficulty agreeing on a candidate. When they proposed Ross Abernathy's name to their colleagues, there was overwhelming approval. The Comptroller of the Currency—with whom such appointments are sometimes discussed in confidence—was clearly pleased; his comment was "I only hope you can get him."

Abernathy was approached—and after a few weeks of negotiations he accepted, joined the bank as "President" two months before the old chairman officially retired and then was elected Chairman and Chief Executive Officer.

Abernathy was then 47. He had started out of high school in a medium-sized bank in Chicago, gotten his bachelor's and master's degree at night at Northwestern while working for the bank, and risen rapidly. Together with another young officer—two years his senior—he had built his bank into a leadership position, first in Chicago, then in the country, then world-wide. And the design and development of the Chicago bank's international business had been entirely his doing, as the other young "comer"—the, like Abernathy an Executive Vice-President—had, by agreement, devoted himself entirely to the domestic and especially the corporate business of the bank. Everybody at the bank knew that the next Chief Executive Officer would be one of the two. And the choice was indeed so narrow that the Board split eight to seven. But the job went to Abernathy's slightly older colleague when the bank's former CEO retired in 1973—and that it was by only one vote did not make the pill any sweeter for the intensely ambitious and competitive Abernathy. He stayed on for one year as Vice-Chairman. Then he left and moved to the city in which Frontier National Bank was located, as chairman and CEO of a group of insurance companies, established but stagnant companies. In three years he had turned them around—and in the process emerged as one of the leaders of the business community in his new home town.

When the Frontier job was offered to him, Abernathy at first hesitated. He had worked terribly hard for three years, and he knew that Frontier would mean even more years of even harder work. He had met a good many Frontier executives and was not impressed by them. And he was not at all sure that Frontier could be turned around. The time to develop what Frontier lacked—that is, especially the large corporate business, the pension-fund business and the international business—seemed to him to have already passed. But then, Frontier had solid assets, especially a very good reputation and old and close ties with leading banks abroad. What, however, persuaded Abernathy to take the job was that he realized that banking was in his blood. He missed the intellectual excitement of banking. He missed the stimulation of the international meetings—of the World Bank, of the International Monetary Fund and so on—and the recognition he had been given at these meetings as one of the brightest younger bankers. And, as he had to admit to himself, the wound inflicted by being passed over in Chicago, still rankled. So he took the job.

He was reasonably clear about what needed being done. But he also knew that he needed a team to do it—and nothing he saw at Frontier made him feel that he had that team there. He could—and did—retire a large number of older executives. That was easy. Frontier, unlike most other large banks, did not retire senior people till they were 70 and, in some cases, continued them until 72. So Abernathy simply had the Board lower the retirement age for everybody to 65. But the younger people serving under these old-timers did not seem to be any different. If anything, they were even more dispirited, even more convinced that "performance" meant taking care of whatever the office boy put into the in-basket and that banking was primarily a matter of belonging to the right country clubs. (Abernathy had never joined one and played tennis because, as he often said, "you can't discuss business over a volley").

And so Abernathy did what he usually did when faced with a major personnel decision. He sought advice. There were three people to whom he usually turned; two were former professors of his, and the third, a lawyer and a member of the law firm that handled his former Chicago bank's legal business. He was not at all surprised when each of them gave him different advice—that was, after all, why he went to them. But he was surprised that he himself could not make up his mind which of the three to listen to—usually Abernathy had little difficulty deciding which advice to follow.

The first man said: "Look, Ross, you really have no choice. You can't fire forty people—you'd have no organization left. You have to develop the small team of top people you need out of the bank's human resources. You, yourself, say that the officers are technically competent. It's up to you to give them vision, to develop performance goals and performance standards and to get them to where they make demands on themselves. Ask a very great deal of them. Make it clear that those who can't or won't live up to these demands will have to go. But also make it clear first that you are willing to support anyone who tries, and secondly, that achievement will be recognized and well rewarded. I don't see what else you can do—I know it means backbreaking work and a lot of disappointment. But there is no other choice, believe me."

The second professor said: "You have no choice, Ross, but to bring in a new top team—not a large one, maybe only half a dozen people but people who know what performance means, and above all, people who know what you mean by performance, people you trust, people you understand, people who trust and understand you. That means people with whom you have worked closely in the past—in large part, of course, young enterprising people from your old Chicago bank. You don't have the time to develop the young MBA's you could hire from the business schools—you have to change the way the bank acts in a hurry. You have to make it clear to the entire bank that there has been a change. And anyone you bring in has to be able to make decisions and to give orders speaking for you, knowing what you are after, and in turn be trusted by you. There is no other choice, believe me."

The lawyer said: "Of course, you have to bring in a new team from the outside. You can't wait until the young hotshots from the B-schools are 'ready' fifteen years hence—by which time the old-timers in Frontier will have corrupted them anyhow. But, Ross, don't bring in your cronies. Bring in only people who have independently, and in banks with which you never had anything to do, proven their capacity to lead and to perform. For one, you will have to be completely objective about them. More important, the bank must feel that the new members of its top management team have been picked for proven performance capacity and not because they are your friends. It should not be hard to find such people. The major banks are full of people who are in the position in which you were in Chicago, that is, just an inch behind a front-runner a few years older but just as good as they are. You can offer them what their present bank cannot offer—a command position and a challenge. But stay away from Chicago. Any place but in Chicago or in the city you are in now. You don't want to raid your local competitors either. There is no other choice, believe me."

Confronted with these three mutually incompatible choices, each presented as inescapable, Abernathy sat down to analyze each alternative. He wrote out three headings: Inside Team; My Team; Outside Strangers. Then he wrote under each heading:
a. Pros/b. Cons/c. Risks/d. Morale problems and morale advantages/ and proceeded to list objectively the arguments for and against each proposed course of action—promising himself to keep opinion and judgment out of the exercise until completing it.

How would you fill out these analysis sheets? Please obey Abernathy's rule and refrain from any expression of preference, any argument and any opinion until you have gone through the complete analysis. And indeed even then.

Case Number 5

The Failed Promotion

An old established and prosperous investment banking firm in New York City decided in the mid-sixties that it needed to strengthen its ability in international business. The firm did not want to go "multinational" itself. The senior partners were convinced that the kind of service they rendered was more akin to a professional practice than to a business and they believed that a professional practice requires fairly small size and close personal contact of the principals. Both the size and contact requirements were, they thought, incompatible with geographically dispersed operations. But they concluded that they needed in the senior management of the firm at least one person with extensive international experience and contacts. He would, they thought, build more or less permanent alliances with investment banks in Europe— perhaps even in Japan—which would enable the firm to acquire both the world-wide expertise and the world-wide banking network it needed to serve its clients.

No such person could be found within the bank. And so, for

the first time in the fifty-year history of the firm, an outsider was brought in directly into a partnership. Frank McQuinn, aged 35, had worked his way up in the international division of one of the big commercial banks. He had started and developed its Düsseldorf branch, moved on to head the large London branch and finally all European operations. McQuinn now wanted to return to the U.S. to live—his children were entering their teens. He knew that in his own bank he would not make it to the very top—he was at the wrong age for that, with a top management team that was itself in their late forties only. He also knew that in his own bank he would have to move into domestic banking to make the next big step— and he loved international work. Also he saw a chance to build an estate in a private banking firm which, though legally incorporated, was, of course, actually a partnership.

So he joined the partnership—and worked out exceedingly well. Within two years he was promoted to senior partner and to membership in the five-man executive committee of the firm. The international business grew very fast and profitably. As a member of the executive committee McQuinn found himself drawn more and more into relationships with major clients in all areas, domestic as well as overseas. The international business grew so fast that he alone could not manage it. Accordingly he discussed with his colleagues on the executive committee the desirability of bringing a second top man into his international department. With their consent in principle, he then picked Stanley Novack as deputy general manager-international, with a clear understanding that Novack would be made a partner if he worked out.

Novack was delighted. In his present position he had little hope of becoming a partner, for that very profitable honor was traditionally reserved to "bankers," that is, to people in charge of client relationships or of operating functions. Novack, while highly respected in the bank, was an analyst—a very successful one— who, at age 31, had become chief of economic and securities analysis and the main advisor to the partners. He was pleased also because it was largely his analysis and recommendation that had pushed the firm into the international field and into bringing in McQuinn. From the first day he had worked closely and well with McQuinn.

But it soon became clear that Novack was not working out as

deputy-head of International. What was wrong was not clear at all, but things just didn't get done. Decisions weren't made, deals were left hanging in mid-air. In short, McQuinn found that he had to do more himself than ever before. After eighteen months of this McQuinn came to the conclusion that Novack had to go. And so he went to the Chairman and Chief Executive Director and said "Novack isn't working out. He has turned out to be no good at all. I am afraid we have to let him go."

The chairman at first said nothing—for a very long time. Then he said gently, "You don't surprise me at all with the news that Novack isn't working out. Indeed I am only surprised that you waited so long before facing up to the disagreeable fact. I expected you in here nine months ago—and I hope you'll learn not to wait so long in the future before facing up to a disagreeable fact. Also," said the Chairman, "I would have been greatly surprised if your decision about staffing International had worked out—regardless of whom you put in there. For you violated all the rules for making promotional decisions. And that's not hindsight. Here," and the chairman pulled out the bottom drawer of his desk and whipped out a memorandum, "is what I wrote to my predecessor on the day you came in here and let me know that you had told Novack that you were going to put him in the job as your deputy."

McQuinn read the memo:

> McQuinn has just been to see me to tell me that he has decided to appoint Stan Novack his deputy and has told this to Novack. I am disturbed, for McQuinn clearly violated the rules you so strongly emphasized for promotions. He settled on a man rather than thinking through the requirements of the job; he settled on one man rather than choosing three or four candidates; and he settled on a man rather than discussing his choice(s) with a number of knowledgeable colleagues. You taught us that a promotion decision made in violation of these rules is almost bound to turn sour—and I have learned the hard way that you are right. Shall I try to get McQuinn to reconsider? I realize I have been amiss in not making sure that McQuinn understands how we in the firm make major people decisions. I am not willing to see Novack destroyed—he is much too valuable a man. But I am reluctant also to overrule McQuinn in a decision within his area, especially one that he has already announced publicly. What is your advice?

And below the former chairman, who was now semi-retired though still a partner had written:

> Keep this memo and wait—but be prepared to bail out both McQuinn *and* Novack!

"So you see, Frank," the chairman went on after McQuinn had read the memo, "I can't say I am surprised that Novack's promotion didn't take. But I am more than surprised, indeed I am shocked, at your attitude. The one thing we know for sure is that you made a mistake—for appointing Novack was your decision. To let Novack go, as you propose, because you made a mistake is not only grossly unfair and unjust. It is asinine. Why should we lose a man as valuable as Novack was all these years, and as achieving as he has been in every previous assignment, just because you made a mistake?"

McQuinn was taken aback. "I don't understand at all," he stammered. "Do you propose to leave Novack in a job he can't manage?"

"Of course not," said the chairman. "He is not doing the job and has to be relieved. We owe that to the firm, but we also owe that to him. But that's only the first and the *easiest* step. I expected you to come into my office first with a considered recommendation on what we should do with Novack now. Where does he belong in this firm? What can he do? What can he not do—and why? Has he, for instance, learned enough about operations through his eighteen months of failure and frustration that we should make him a partner in charge of analysis and research—something we have never done since we felt analysts didn't know enough to become partners? Should we move him into a totally different area? If so, which one? With whom should he work? Should he continue to work with you, or not? That's your responsiblity—you put a performing man into the wrong position."

"And then," continued the chairman, "I expected you to come in and tell me why you think that Novack has not worked out. After all, he did well in every previous assignment he has had—and now he fails. That needs explanation and you are the responsible man, the one who owes this explanation to the firm, to yourself, and, most of all, to Stan Novack."

McQuinn sat silently for several minutes. Clearly he had difficulty taking in what he had heard. Then he said slowly, "I can see why you expect me to think through what we should be doing with Novack and why you reject my hasty conclusion that we have to let him go. And I am grateful to you for teaching me something I should have seen myself. But I am totally baffled by your second request. Isn't it clear what happened? Novack was promoted to a job that turned out to be beyond him, that's all."

"So you believe in the Peter Principle," said the chairman, with considerable sharpness. "Frank, believe me, that's nothing but an alibi for a lazy or incompetent executive—and I don't think you want to be either. There isn't the slightest reason to believe that a person who has performed well in a number of assignments will all of a sudden fail to perform in another assignment because he has reached his level of incompetence, whatever that may mean. On the contrary, it's far more likely that people who perform in a number of assignments will perform in the next one—performance is performance, after all."

"If they don't, there's got to be a reason. Once in a while the reason may be that they stop performing, stop working, get old, sick or tired, burn out. But I don't think that's what happened to Stan Novack. It's far more likely that the reason was one of the three common reasons why promotions fail—all three primarily boss-failure rather than man-failure. Either the promoted man keeps on doing what he did in the old assignment oblivious to the fact that it's a new assignment and requires doing different things. And that happens always because the boss does not pull up the man, does not require of him that he think through what the new job requires. Remember when you came here first how we called you before the executive committee—three times at ninety-day intervals—and asked you to think through and let us know what your new job with us required of you? And every time you kind of asked us for guidance and we said, 'The only thing we are willing and able to tell you is that the new job requires different things from what the job you had at the commercial bank required.' Remember? Have you done this for Novack, or did you let him continue to do good analysis such as he had been doing for years? If so, don't blame Novack, blame yourself. You didn't do your part in making your promotional decision effective."

"Or have we learned that Novack is an analyst and temperamentally unable to hold a decision-making leadership position? Till you put him in as your deputy he always acted as an analyst and adviser. Other people made the decisions. Maybe he just cannot take the burden of decisions. It's not uncommon. Even people as young as Novack can't always learn—it's a matter of personality as much as of knowledge or skill. And finally, perhaps the job you created and into which you put Novack, is an impossible job, a job no one can do. A job, for instance, in which a person must fail if he does what the boss used to do, but is also a failure if he does anything else. Or it may be a job in which he has to be both an assistant to and the actual head of the operation."

"You have two weeks," said the chairman, "to think through first what you recommend the firm should do with Stan Novack. We have to pull him out, and I shall do so today by asking him to take on an assignment for me, but in two weeks you have to make a recommendation. And it had better start out with the realization that a decision of yours has failed to pan out. And then, within two weeks I also expect a reasoned and well-supported analysis of why Stan Novack didn't work out. Was it your failure to give him the guidance you should have given him? Was it the wrong temperament? Then we will both know what kind of job Novack can take in the future and also what kind of person we need for the job you want to fill. Or do we have to redesign the job so that human beings can fill it? We have no right to ask people to take on jobs that will defeat them, no right to break good people. We don't have enough good young people to practice human sacrifice.

"Until you have thought through the reason why Novack's promotion failed, I shall not permit you to appoint anyone in Novack's place."

What do you think of the chairman's argument? What do you think of the rules for making a promotional decision which the former chairman had worked out? How could McQuinn go about answering the chairman's request and find out the reasons why Novack's promotion had failed?

Case Number 6

The Invincible
Life Assurance Company

The Invincible Life Assurance Company was, almost in the literal sense, the child of Philip Mulholland. He had founded the company shortly after World War I when he was a young insurance salesman who had become convinced that a locally-owned and locally-managed company could give better service to the rapidly growing mid-western region than any of the established big life insurance companies in the east. He had built the company over the years, first into the leading life underwriter of its own territory, then into one of the leading companies in the nation. He had been a pioneer in developing new forms of insurance. Both group-life insurance and employee pension plans were first sold and developed in the territory by the Invincible, for instance.

If the Invincible was Mulholland's child, it was also his life. During the first ten or twelve years of its existence, he literally lived in the office. Even weekends he spent mostly visiting salesmen, establishing new agencies or personally settling claims. He had married in his twenties, but his wife's death after a few years of happy marriage left him lonely, a widower, and childless. And from then on to the end of his life his whole existence turned around the Invincible. The last twenty years of his life he lived in a simple hotel suite three blocks away from the office, and he went to the hotel only to sleep.

Mulholland was a quiet man, held in respect and affection by everyone who knew him. When he died, it was no surprise to his friends to hear that he had given away most of his money to charity during his lifetime and that he had left his modest estate to establish scholarships for the education of his employees' children. Even though the company had long grown to large size, he kept his small and unassuming office. He was particularly interested in helping younger people and used to spend long hours discussing their problems (and the challenge of life insurance) with whatever bright youngsters he would notice when walking through the office. In fact, American life insurance is sprinkled with "Mulholland's young men," people whom he had found, had trained, and had finally found positions for; and among them are some of the biggest names in American insurance today.

Yet, these very qualities resulted in total lack of order and organization in the company. Mulholland never boasted that he could do every job in an insurance company better than anyone else. Yet, everybody in the company was well aware that this was indeed the case. Also the company had grown imperceptively—and to Mr. Mulholland it was still the small office in which he had started, alone with a rate table and a battered typewriter. As a result, all major—and most minor—decisions still automatically went up to him. He decided on salaries, for instance, for everybody, from office boys on up. There was officially an "Underwriting Committee" to pass on doubtful applications or on policies in excess of $25,000; the State Insurance Commissioners had insisted on such a committee. But the district sales managers usually "cleared" such policies with Mr. Mulholland on the telephone directly; and while Mulholland always intended to "bring it up" at the next committee meeting, he rarely did so. In fact, vacancies on the committee often went for years without being filled. New insurance policies and contracts—the "new products" of the life insurance business—Mr. Mulholland always worked out himself, using the actuarial department only to do the mechanical computations for him. And he personally looked over and decided every appointment or promotion. As a result, his executives were never allowed to do any but purely specialist work—and primarily routine work operating along the lines determined by Mr. Mulholland himself.

Even worse were the results of his kindness, and of his interest in young people. As the company prospered, Mr. Mulholland became very generous to the old-timers who had worked with him in the early days. Salaries in the company were a strict secret—only Mr. Mulholland knew what people were being paid. But it was an open secret that in every department there were old-timers whose salary was quite a bit higher than that of their superior. Also in every department there were bright young men who had come to Mr. Mulholland's attention, who were being used by him—usually without telling the department head—for special assignments and who were often being paid for these assignments separately and in undisclosed amounts. Titles were used by Mr. Mulholland as a reward for special services rather than as indication of work and rank—with the result that there were about 25 vice presidents who reported to men who themselves did not have vice-presidential rank and title. And since Mr. Mulholland himself made all decisions, practically every man who carried any responsibility reported to him directly rather than to the department head. The number of men who were only accountable to the President—in name or in fact—had never been determined but was running close to a hundred.

As long as Mulholland lived, this worked fine. But Mr. Mulholland, the founder of the Invincible, and the only president and chairman it had ever had, died suddenly on Labor Day, 1970, a few weeks before his 77th birthday and the fiftieth anniversary of the founding of the company.

The Board of Directors met a few days later and unanimously, almost without discussion, elected James Wintress as the new President.

This was not much of a surprise to anyone in the company, except to Mr. Wintress himself. Wintress had, for fifteen years, been head of the Investment Department. He was not the oldest of the senior vice presidents, but the youngest . But since the others were all seventy or more, that made him the only possible candidate in the group. Also he was the only department head who had really managed; for Mr. Mulholland knew that he himself lacked financial experience and left the investment decisions to this investment vice president. Wintress also was the one officer of the company who had any outside business experience; before joining Invincible as a Senior Securities Analyst in 1948, he had been a Trust Officer of an important bank. Finally Wintress was the only vice president who was at all known to the Board members, since Mulholland had left the presentation of investment recommendations for Board decision to him.

Wintress himself was, however, quite surprised, and by no means only agreeably. He knew that none of the other senior men were young enough to be given the presidency. But at 63 he considered himself far too old. Also he knew very little about any phase of life insurance except investment—Mulholland's way of operations had ensured that functions were quite isolated from one another—and in particular knew nothing about selling insurance, handling claims, and working out new policies. Indeed, Wintress had expected to retire in another two years when, under the Company's policy, he had the right to retire with three-quarters of his salary (there was no compulsory retirement age, nor any annuity plan).

Wintress himself was fully prepared to be asked by the Board for his recommendation how to fill the job. He had decided to urge that the new president be found on the outside among the many "Mulholland young men" who had made good after leaving the Invincible. In fact, he had several names in mind.

One reason for this recommendation—which he was never asked to make—was his awareness of the organizational chaos in the company. He figured that some one who had grown up in the Invincible and been trained by Mulholland, would understand and appreciate the spirit of the place and the achievement of the old man, would respect and maintain both and would not ruthlessly or carelessly hurt people and spirit in reorganizing the company. Yet, he thought, such a man, accustomed to better organized companies, would know that the company needed radical reorganization. Finally, he figured that the men he had in mind—who were in their mid-forties or early fifties—were young enough to carry through the big reorganization task that had to be faced.

What decided him, after all, to accept the offer of the presidency despite his age and relative inexperience was precisely his concern with the reorganization of the company and with the difficult and painful decisions on people that had to be taken. He figured that the company could run along pretty nicely for five years on the technical and functional competence it had to a high degree. That he did not know too much about these functions would not matter too much, therefore. At the same time he would have five years to put the organizational house in order and to leave a manageable company to his successor. And five years, he decided and made clear to the Board, would be the maximum time span for which he would serve.

After having accepted, Wintress, however, began to wonder how precisely he should go about the organization job. He felt he could not discuss his qualms with any of his Directors, if only because that would have implied criticizing the dead Mulholland, and by implication the Board of Directors, who had let him operate the way he did. He also felt strongly that he could not discuss the matter with any of his officers, as this was bound to get "on the grapevine" and to upset the entire company. He, therefore, decided to seek the advice of an old friend, who had started out with him in the securities business forty years ago and who had, in the meantime, risen to become senior partner of an important investment banking firm. Mr. Amasa Gray was known to be a deep student of organization, and had himself successfully reorganized many an industrial company. And he could be depended upon to be both discreet and disinterested.

After listening for a couple of days, Gray summed up his advice in these words:

> You know very well that you can't finish the organization job in five years. You will have to make far too many compromises with personalities, traditions, and decency for that. Also, no organization job is better than the understanding and support of the people in the organization—and you can't change habits and attitudes of the old-timers that fast. You also know that the time is short for the standard remedies such as starting manager development of your young people—that's one of the things that won't bear fruit in less than ten or fifteen years and you have at most five. Yet you know that you need real results—and need them fast. Not only are you going to need a successor in five years. Most of your executives are older than you are and will need being replaced much sooner— yet you have no one to replace them with, and don't even know which people should be replaced, which jobs should be maintained and what the qualifications for the candidates should be. What you have to do is to work out a *basic approach* that clearly expresses the basic principles of organization, job structure, and staffing you believe to be right for the company. With these principles, no compromising can be allowed—you have to be ruthless in sticking to them, if necessary. And you have to do enough actual reorganization, actual abolishing of jobs, actual straightening out of salaries, actual building of new functions and new organs to make clear to everyone in the company what you are after and that you mean business. First you have to work out the approach. Then you have to decide what action measures you are going to take

right away and why. After you have done this, you must discuss
the plan with your Board and with your top officers. And then you
can—and probably should—also bring in outside help. But until
you have done this thinking job, you can only do harm by talking
about it or by bringing in experts. And this thinking job only you
can do. Give yourself three months to think through your approach and decide on basic principles—and forget until then all
considerations of tradition, practicality, people, tactics and so
forth. I'll be very happy to sit down with you again after you have
decided on the principles of your approach and plan; until then,
even I could not help you very much.

Mr. Wintress was not exactly happy to hear this. He had hoped to
be told how to do the job rather than what the job was. He was,
however, honest enough to admit to himself that Gray was right—
this was the president's job and one that could not be unloaded or
delegated. Still, he had doubts. On the one hand he felt that Gray
was not ambitious enough in his thinking, and that to have nothing
but an approach within five years was not good enough. At the
same time, he also felt that Gray was too demanding—
"impersonal" he called it in his mind—with his requirement of "no
compromise on principles whatever the personalities or human
considerations involved." On the whole, however, he was impressed with Gray's argument. And so, after a few days of doubt, he
sat down to figure out for himself what a right approach to the reorganization of the Invincible Life Assurance Company might be.

Where should Wintress start in his thinking? Are there any
things Wintress could do that would surely be wrong and could
not work? Are there any things Wintress could do that would
surely be both right and relevant to his to his problems?

PART SIX

MANAGERIAL SKILLS

Case Number 1

Lyndon Johnson's Decision

When Lyndon Johnson was Senate Majority leader during the Eisenhower years, he was adamantly opposed to any American involvement in Indo-China. It was widely believed that it was his opposition which, in 1954 after the French defeat in Vietnam, made Eisenhower rule out any American military intervention against the strong pressure for it on the part of his Secretary of State, John Foster Dulles, his Vice President, Richard Nixon, and his Chairman of the Joint Chiefs of Staff, Admiral Radford. Johnson continued his opposition to any American involvement in Indo-China when he became President Kennedy's Vice President. He was outspoken about his desire to withdraw the American advisors whom Eisenhower had sent to bolster the South Vietnamese regime; and he strongly opposed the plunge into Vietnamese politics on the part of the Kennedy Administration when, in the fall of 1963—shortly before President Kennedy's assassination—it countenanced the coup against President Diem and thereby made the American government the guarantor of the successor regime, and the actual power in South Vietnam. Johnson continued this position after becoming President and resisted all through 1964 pressures for increased American involvement, especially from the Foreign and Defense Secretaries he had inherited from Mr. Kennedy. He strongly emphasized during his election campaign of 1964 his resistance to any attempt to expand the war in Vietnam or to make it an American war. Indeed, his opposition to our involvement in Vietnam was so great and so well known that it was widely feared in the Pentagon and the State Department—and even more in Saigon—that Johnson was encouraging the North Vietnamese to attack by, in effect, promising them that the U.S. would not resist.

Then, in the spring of 1965, Hanoi adopted a new and aggressive policy. Previously, Hanoi had confined itself to supporting insurgents in South Vietnam—with arms, advisors, and money. It had, in other words, matched the American policy of support for the South Vietnamese government and also the American decision not to become involved militarily on a large scale. Beginning in the spring of 1965—only a few weeks after Johnson was sworn in for his second term—North Vietnam began to send North Vietnamese Regulars, heavily armed with Russian armor and artillery into South Vietnam, where they took over military operations from the South Vietnamese Viet Cong guerrillas. In late spring these North Vietnamese troops—by now the equivalent of about fifteen American divisions—launched a massive attack clearly aimed at cutting South Vietnam in two. North Vietnam's objective suddenly seemed to be a "military solution," that is, the defeat and destruction of the South Vietnamese military. In the face of this situation, Johnson changed his basic position. He decided that force had to be met with force. He sent a major American military force to Vietnam to take over the main burden of fighting the North Vietnamese. He argued—enough documents have been published to make this clear—that the South Vietnamese would not rise to join the North Vietnamese, as indeed they did not. In this situation a defeat of

Hanoi's military thrust would rapidly induce Hanoi to re-establish the uneasy truce that had prevailed before, if not to replace it, as had happened in Korea ten years earlier, with a long-term armistice. Militarily the U.S. was at first fully successful. The North Vietnamese were beaten back with very heavy losses in manpower and almost complete loss of their equipment. By fall of 1965, the North Vietnamese were in full retreat, pulling their badly mauled divisions back into North Vietnam. There was every reason to believe that Johnson's basic premise, that such a defeat would lead to a valid armistice, would be proven right. We know that active negotiations via Moscow were going on and that around Christmas, 1965, an armistice was thought "to be in the bag" in Moscow, apparently as well as in Washington.

What happened then we do not know. One theory is that Brezshnev, until then only one of the three top men in the Soviet hierarchy, made his bid for supreme power in late 1965 and needed the support of the military (and it seems, especially of the Navy) which he only got by turning "hawk." To support this theory there is the fact that Russia began suddenly to step up military supplies to Hanoi—after telling Hanoi and the world in 1965 that supplies would be limited to replacement of lost equipment; that at the same time the Soviet Union, after long hesitation, decided on a crash program to build a three-ocean navy; and that it took over supplying India with arms on a massive scale. Another theory argues that the balance of power in Hanoi, between "doves" and "hawks," shifted decisively toward the "hawks," as Ho Chi Minh suffered a heart attack or stroke and could no longer control events (though he did not die until 1969). Another theory—the least likely one, by the way—maintains that growing American resistance to the Vietnamese war encouraged the Communists; but there was still very little resistance to the Vietnamese war in this country in early 1966, though it was beginning to grow and to be more vocal.

In any event, by January or February, 1966, it had become clear that events were not following Lyndon Johnson's expectations. Hanoi had broken off truce negotiations. Instead it was pouring back supplies and men into South Vietnam. The Russians who, only a few months earlier, had acted as intermediaries between Washington and Hanoi were stepping up their support for Hanoi and refusing to use their influence to persuade Hanoi to moderate its demands for total surrender. And so President Johnson had to face the fact that his policy, despite its resounding military success, had been a political failure.

When he sat down with his advisors—mostly the crew he had inherited two years earlier from President Kennedy—no one felt very good about the situation. But prevailing sentiment—and Johnson agreed reluctantly—was that there was really no choice but to hang on. It was now clear that the North Vietnamese could not win a military victory against American forces. It was equally clear that the South Vietnamese, while perhaps not enthusiastic about their regime, did not support the North Vietnamese government. So, the consensus ran, "sooner or later" Hanoi or their "real master," Moscow, would have to see the futility of the drive for a "military solution:" and until then all the U.S. could do was to hang on.

No one liked this conclusion. But every one—Rusk, McNamara, McGeorge Bundy, the Joint Chiefs of Staff—went along, reluctantly. The only dissenter in the group, according to all reports, was George Ball, Undersecretary of State. He was primarily concerned with economic affairs, and until then, very far away from the Vietnam problem. Ball is reported to have said: "I don't know, Mr. President, what the right answer is. But I do know that continuing last year's policy is the wrong thing to do. It cannot work and must end in disaster. For it violates basic principles of decision-making."

1) What principles did Ball have in mind?

2) Would you agree with what is said to have been Ball's point, i.e., that there are "principles" of decision-making and that to violate them dooms the decision?

Case Number 2

The
New Export Manager

Ever since it was founded in 1924, the Ridgewood Tool Company—a leading manufacturer of hand tools—had been in the export business. For many years an exporting firm in New York City had had the exclusive distribution of the company's products outside of the U.S. Then, as exports grew, the company appointed distributors or agents in various foreign countries. An export manager was appointed in 1956; but he was mainly a clerk handling incoming orders from overseas and arranging for the collection, through the company's bank, of the monies due. By 1970, however, the company's export volume had grown to the point where this did not work any more. And when the old export manager retired, management decided that the export business had to be properly managed and had also to be properly organized. Maybe, one of the directors mused, the company even had to set up its own facility in Germany, where the company's products were well known and popular. But there was no one in the company who knew anything about foreign business; and so a young, energetic fellow—Frank Andrews, aged 35—was hired from International General Electric to become the new export manager. Andrews made a quick trip to visit the company's main foreign distributors and agents. Upon his return he told the President of the company that he would work out a plan for the company's foreign business. And then he retired to his office. He appointed a veteran clerk in the export department as Assistant Export Manager and gave him the job of handling the day-to-day business, which proceeded along at its accustomed donkey trot.

But what did Andrews himself do? He was at the office every day. People peeping through his office door—which he kept tightly closed most of the time—saw big stacks of books, papers, and reports, behind which Andrew's head was barely visible. BUT WHAT DID HE DO?

After this had been going on for about four months, pressure on the President began to mount to the point where he called Andrews into his office and said, "You have been here almost half a year— and none of us can figure out what you are doing." Andrews was clearly surprised. "Don't you see that I am studying," he came back. "And until I can come in to you with a proper plan, what's the point in my wasting your time." "Mr. Andrews," the President said, "you and we clearly made a mistake. I think it would be better if you looked for a job elsewhere."

The President, when he recounts this experience, confesses himself totally nonplussed. "The fellow came to us with a reputation as a dynamic, take-charge, live-wire," he says. "And clearly he must have something. Since leaving us, he has joined a very big company and is now their Vice President for Europe and, I hear, doing very well. But he spent six months with us just sitting and doing nothing."

Andrews is not only nonplussed but still quite bitter. "These old fogies," he says, "just didn't realize that one has to plan an international business. They had no figures, no plans, no organization. They didn't hire me to peddle pliers but to get them into the world market the right way. What did they expect me to do except to work out the right plan?"

But one day when he said that to an old friend—an experienced lawyer with whom he had gone to college—he got an unexpected reply: "Sure, Frank," the friend said, "these people were 'old fogies'. But the fault was yours—you acted like a young, arrogant fool."

Can you explain to Andrews what his lawyer friend meant? And then, can you perhaps think through what the company and its President might have done to prevent what clearly was a total breakdown of communications?

Case Number 3

Who is the Brightest
Hamster in the Laboratory?

Wickstrom Pharmaceuticals started in the late nineteenth century in a small town in Northern Minnesota when Sven Wickstrom, recently arrived from his native Sweden, began to sell herb teas and simple Swedish folk remedies to the many Scandinavian farmers who were then streaming into Minnesota. His son built up a small business on this basis—mostly cough medicines, soothing syrups for teething babies, and the like. But the business, never a great success, began to languish in the 1930s when prescriptions by physicians and widely-advertised national brands of patent medicines took over. Brian Wickstrom, the grandson of the founder, was well aware of this; and as a boy, growing up in Minneapolis, he vowed to leave both Minnesota and the family business as soon as he could. However, just as he had finished high school, he was drafted into the army to fight in World War II. When he came back he used his G.I. benefits to go to college, majoring in business and intending to get a job with a big company. But, within a few weeks of his graduation in 1948, his father died and his mother asked him to take over the family business if only to salvage whatever little money there might be. Brian took over—for six months.

But before the six months were up he found, to his great surprise, that the business, while having absolutely no saleable products, had excellent manufacturing facilities in a small but modern plant; his father had put all the revenue into machinery and into a first-rate lab. Manufacturing capacity in the pharmaceutical industry was scarce in those years. And so Brian bid on and got lucrative sub-contracts from major pharmaceutical manufacturers who were just then beginning to move into mass-production of the "wonder drugs," especially the then brand-new antibiotics. In no time, Wickstrom was making money—and Brian found that he enjoyed running the business. But he also knew that he had to have products—and that meant he had to have a business strategy and to do a good deal of research and product development.

During his war-time service, Brian had known and come to like another young G.I.—the same age but of totally different background. Fritz Hirschland had come to the United States with his family as a refugee from Hitler's persecution of the Jews when he was just about to enter junior high. He had finished his secondary schooling in the United States, fully intending to become a physician like five generations of Hirschlands before him. Instead, he was drafted—about the same time as Brian Wickstrom—right after high-school graduation. A year later, in Officers Training Camp, he met Wickstrom and they became fast friends. They went through the war and then on to college together. But while Wickstrom went back to Minnesota to rescue the family business, Hirschland (who by that time had switched to biochemistry) went on to graduate school, fully intent on an academic career. Wickstrom's problems intrigued him, however. And so, while still working on his Ph.D. he got more and more involved in Wickstrom Chemical—and as soon as he had received the degree he took the job as Research Director of Wickstrom Chemical and as the scientifiic partner in a team of which Brian was the business partner. It was Brian who thought through the strategy and defined the mission and objectives of a rapidly growing specialty producer in the pharmaceutical industry. But it was Hirschland who understood the scientific opportunities and identified the products the company should concentrate on to get leadership position in small but important—and lucrative—areas. Altogether, Hirschland proved himself both an outstanding research scientist in his own right—and brilliant in adapting a new pharmaceutical to specific clinical uses—and a first-class research manager, particularly in his ability to bring together and lead a team of young, enthusiastic, and performing scientists.

Brian Wickstrom, who had always been the very picture of youthful health and energy, was felled by cancer when barely yet fifty. Every one assumed that Hirschland would succeed him. But Hirschland said "No." "I belong in the lab, and anyhow we have a better qualified chief executive in Charlie Swansford, our administrative v.p. and general counsel." And so the job went to Swansford, a few years younger than either Wickstrom or Hirschland. He had started as a patent lawyer and then successfully become general counsel and administrative v.p. in charge of law, patents, administration, finance and personnel. While not as close to Hirschland as Wickstrom had been, he had become a good friend—and it was to Hirschland he had been coming with his growing concern over the lack of professional management and proper organization in the last years of Wickstrom's life. "The company has outgrown Wickstrom's gung-ho style," he used to complain, "we are too big and too complex to be run by any one's intuition, no matter how brilliant he is." And Hirschland, for all his affection for Wickstrom, had to agree—indeed it was precisely Swansford's concern with, and expertise in, management that made him in Hirschland's eyes the ideal successor to Wickstrom.

Hirschland was delighted when Swansford rapidly reorganized manufacturing and marketing and when he brought in a strong, capable chief financial man. And he applauded when Swansford, a year later, instituted formal budgeting and planning—for one-year, three-years and five years ahead. But he balked when Swansford asked him to make and submit budgets for research. "You. can't budget research," he said. "What we do does not depend on our decision. It depends on how a lot of hamsters and guinea pigs in the lab react when we inject some stuff under their skins or feed it to them. If they react one way, we triple or quadruple what we spend—as fast as we can spend it. And if they react another way we cut back and drop a whole line of research and don't spend any money on it."

"Alright, Fritz," said Swansford, after Hirschland had made this little speech the umpteenth time, "if that's the case, why don't you write out your resignation as research director and nominate the brightest hamster in your lab to be your successor. If the hamster makes the budget decisions, then he rather than you manages research—and you know that it is only good management to make sure that authority and responsibility go together."

Hirschland, who thought this terribly funny, laughed until he had tears in his eyes. But when he had calmed down, Swansford continued: "I am only half joking, Fritz. If you can't or won't budget, we'll have to get someone who can and will. It's not that the company needs to know what the research budget is—we could probably manage from one surprise to the next the way we have. But research needs to have a budget; a budget is *your* tool. Without it, you cannot properly anticipate your decisions, cannot properly weigh alternatives, cannot properly decide whether you and your high-performing people are assigned the right jobs, and whether you have assigned the right people, and enough of them, to get results. You won't come out with hard and fast figures—and, of course, one can and should always change a budget if the situation changes. But you have to have a starting place. I don't think your hamsters *do* make your decisions—but if they really do, then we'd just have to teach *them* to budget—though I'd rather you did it."

Hirschland was not convinced—but he had respect for Swansford. He was also intrigued by Swansford's insistence that the budget was a tool for the manager. He had always conceived of a budget as something top management and the financial people needed and required *from* the manager. "But where," he asked as he rose to leave, "do I begin? Where might I and my research people get anything out of budgeting?"

Where could Dr. Hirschland start, and in what areas of his work might budgeting help him the most?

Case Number 4

The Insane
Junior High School Principal

When the new city council of a well-known Eastern suburb appointed a new school board (in the East many school boards are appointive still), it gave it one mandate: eliminate the extreme racial segregation in our public schools. In 1945, at the end of World War II, the town had been lily-white; then the black influx began—mostly black middle class fleeing the ghettos of the neighboring big city. By 1966 the town had a black population of 40 per cent. But apart from the consolidated senior high school whose 4500 students contained a black minority of 30 per cent, all schools in the town were strictly segregated—achieved mostly through dividing the school districts to fit segregated housing patterns. The worst cases were the five junior-high schools. Four had big new buildings but their facilities were grossly under-utilized; indeed they were half-empty. And they were almost completely white. The fifth was a swollen monstrosity, running double shifts in an old, condemned, rickety building that had been slated to be torn down even before World War II; and it exceeded the State's fire and occupancy maxima by 50 to 60 per cent in every room and on every shift. It was solidly black.

The new board set to work with a will. But it soon found itself up against serious resistance—almost sabotage—on the part of the black community. The very people who had screamed the loudest about racial segregation in the schools seemed unwilling to do anything—including the three highly respected black members of the seven-man board. Slowly and with great reluctance, the black members hinted at the problem. Everybody knew, of course, that the fifth, the black junior high would be closed and its students redistributed to the four newer, empty and so far, white schools. Even so, these schools would only be moderately filled. Everybody knew that one junior high school principal would be kicked upstairs—probably into a job as assistant principal of the high school or assistant superintendent at the district level. All the white members assumed that Mr. Milgram, aged 62 and principal of one of the white schools, would be promoted, that is be made to vacate the principalship. After all, he was within three years of retirement and altogether not the strongest principal in the system. But everybody in the black community knew something no one in the white community even suspected. Mrs. Wicks, the black principal of the black junior high, was suffering from advanced mental illness. Where for years she had been "eccentric," her condition had worsened rapidly to the point where she was a raving maniac half the time—a pretty advanced case of paranoia with violent episodes. Indeed, several years earlier, the black community had quietly taken steps to make sure that the poor woman would never be alone but would always be surrounded by a few sturdy, sensible and reliable women members of the black community—this was after she had attacked one of her teachers with a pair of scissors and cut her severely around the wrist and the neck. But Mrs. Wicks was the only black

131

principal in the town. In fact, she was the only black principal in the state and as such a symbol of black achievement and a by-word in every black home. Yet, should the School Board have to reassign the principals, they would have—according to state law—to appear in person before the Board, undergo questioning, develop their plan for the school they were applying for, and spend a gruelling four to five hours with the School Board. The sessions of the School Board were public, well attended, and rather stormy, especially as the residents of one part of town—the part where Mr. Milgram's junior high was situated—were known to be strongly opposed to racial integration, determined to fight it, and certain to make things mighty unpleasant for a black candidate for the principalship of a "white" junior high. That Mrs. Wicks could get through such a session without getting out of control seemed most unlikely.

The problem "solved" itself. On a Sunday, at church service, the woman who had been detailed to watch poor Mrs. Wicks ceased to pay attention for a few minutes. Mrs. Wicks suddenly whipped out a butcher's knife, ran up to the altar, and attacked the black minister, stabbing him twice in the back. He survived; but, of course, she had to be hospitalized, and had to be removed from her job.

But the Saturday night before that, one of the black members of the School Board—himself a respected physician in the community with a practice that antedated the black influx of the post-war period and was largely white middle-class—had taken the bull by the horns and had called a meeting of the Board in his home. "Look," he said, "you people ought to know why we are dragging our feet—you ought to know about the problem with Mrs. Wicks. All of us on the Board, black and white, have a communications problem. The black community does not really trust us to keep all the black teachers at Mrs. Wicks' junior high when we close it—even though they know that we will need just as many teachers as before, if not more. But that we will really, in the face of resistance from Mr. Milgram's district, move black teachers into white, or formerly white, schools and give them the same jobs and the same opportunities— that's even hard for me to believe and very hard for any other black. But that we are then going to appoint another black principal to one of the four schools, that no black community in this country can believe—and you know we'll face opposition from a good many whites who will at least urge us to wait until Milgram reaches retirement age in three years. Mrs. Wicks is a very, very sick woman—we in the black community all know this. But still she made it when it wasn't easy—and all of us have been used for years to look at her with pride. What do you plan to do to communicate our commitment to integration, not only of students but of faculties and administrators?"

What would you answer?

Case Number 5

The Structure of a Business Decision

The Nakamura Lacquer Company of Kyoto, Japan was one of the many hundred small handicraft shops making lacquer ware for the daily table use of the Japanese people when the American GI's of the Occupation Army began to buy lacquer ware as souvenirs. Young Mr. Nakamura, who in 1948 had just taken over the old family business, saw therein an opportunity, but soon found that traditional handicraft methods were both too slow and too expensive to supply this new demand. He developed ways of introducing simple methods of machine-coating, machine-polishing, and machine-inspection into what had been purely a handicraft, carried out with the simplest tools. And while the American GI and his souvenir-hunting disappeared with the American Occupation in 1952, Nakamura built a substantial business, employing several thousand men, and produced 500,000 sets of lacquer table ware each year for the Japanese mass-consumer market. The Nakamura "Chrysanthemum" brand has become Japan's best-known and best-selling brand—good quality, middle-class, and dependable. Outside of Japan, however, Nakamura did practically no business, except for selling occasionally to American tourists through his established Japanese outlets such as the big department stores.

This was the situation when, early in 1960—with U.S. interest in things Japanese beginning to grow—Mr. Nakamura received in rapid sequence two visitors from the United States, both very highly recommended and equipped with the very highest and best credentials.

"Mr. Nakamura," the first one said, "I am Phil Rose of the National China Company—V.P. Marketing. As you probably know, we are the largest manufacturer of good-quality dinner ware in the United States with our "Rose & Crown" brand, which accounts for almost 30 per cent of total sales. We think that we can successfully introduce lacquer dinner ware to a small but discriminating public in the U.S. We have investigated the Japanese industry and found that you are by far the best and most modern producer. We are willing to give you a firm order for three years for annual purchases of 400,000 sets of your lacquer dinner ware at 5 per cent more, delivered in Japan, than your Japanese jobbers pay you, provided the merchandise is made for us with our trade mark "Rose & Crown," and provided that you undertake not to sell anyone else in the U.S. lacquer ware either with your brand or with any other brand during that period."

Mr. Nakamura had scarcely recovered from this shock when the next visitor appeared. "I am Walter Semmelbach," he said, "Semmelback, Semmelbach and Whittacker, Chicago—largest supplier of hotel and restaurant supplies in the States, and buyers of dinner ware and similar goods for a number of department stores. We think we can successfully introduce good-quality Japanese lacquer dinner ware to our market. In fact, all our customers are willing to try it out. We think there is a market for at least 600,000 sets a year. Within five years it should be a couple of millions. We have investigated your industry and feel you are the only man in Japan who can exploit this opportunity. Now we know your government does not allow you to invest any money abroad; we don't ask you for a penny. We are willing to pay the full costs of introduction. We are willing to budget $1,500,000 for the next two years for introduction and promotion. You don't owe us that money. All we ask of you is (A) that we get the exclusive representation for your "Chrysanthemum" brand for five years at standard commission rates, and (B) that the first 20 percent on all the sales we make during that time—which we figure is roughly YOUR profit margin—be used to pay off the money we actually spend for promotion and introduction as certified by a firm of independent accountants we want you to name."

Assume that both men are bona-fide, and that both check out as first-rate connections to have. Mr. Nakamura, therefore, has to think the offers through seriously—but what is it he has to think through? What decision is he being asked to make? How indeed can one compare the two offers?

Case Number 6

The
Corporate Control Panel

The new President and CEO of a large multinational chemical company had come up through the legal and financial areas. When he joined the company, after Navy service in World War II, it had been small and regional, if not local. He first realized that its rapid growth required very different legal approaches to those his predecessor as house counsel had used; and his legal draftsmanship and legal advice were largely instrumental in enabling the company to grow into a big business. Then he had taken over as the company's chief financial officer, just when the multinational expansion of the 1960s was getting under way. Again he had realized that the existing financial structure and, even more, the existing financial information and control, had been outgrown; and again his leadership in developing far more sophisticated information systems had a lot to do with the smooth and rapid growth of the company, and with its ability to integrate companies, especially European companies, smoothly into its structure after acquisition or merger.

But when the same man became Chief Executive Officer, around 1967 or so, he was dismayed at the paper load that descended on him every working day. He believed firmly that a CEO has to be in close touch with people; he believed even more firmly that he had to have time to visit key people outside company headquarters, especially the key people in the overseas affiliates which accounted, by 1976, for almost 50 per cent of the company's sales and profits and were growing faster than the U.S. business. And here he was chained to a desk and buried under figures and reports. That he himself, only a few years ago, had initiated most of these figures and reports and had been highly praised for doing so, only added insult to the injury.

For a year he tried to do both, stay on top of the paper flood *and* manage the company—only to come to the conclusion that he did neither. He spent hours with the reports, to be sure; but he did not really understand what they were telling him and felt strongly that he was losing control. He also neglected the business, and above all, the people. When his most achieving research director quit and stated bluntly as his reason that he was not getting enough top-management time and attention, the CEO knew that he had to do something drastic.

Then he remembered Christine Tschudi—a young Swiss woman who had started in the French affiliate and had risen to controller there in a short time; who had then put in for a transfer to New York headquarters as she wanted to get an advanced degree in information and control systems and had written her Ph.D thesis on "The Corporate Control Panel" (the CEO had gotten a presentation copy and had laid it aside as he didn't understand a word of it, or rather there weren't many words in it. It was all equations, it seemed)—who now served as Assistant Controller for the company's overseas affiliates and rapidly making a name for herself. He called in Christine Tschudi and said "I need a control panel, and I need it fast. It has to give us in top management all the information we need to have control of the company; it has to give us the information fast enough for us to take action—most of what I get is history by the time I get it; all of us in top management and top operating management have to get the same information and know what we are talking about; it has to highlight the areas where important things happen or do not happen so that we know what to focus on; and it has to be concise enough so that I can understand it by studying it one day a month and so that we can reach agreement on where action or study are required in a two to three-day session each month—a session which it will be your job to prepare. Don't rush," said the CEO; "I know I can't get it tomorrow, but I do expect a pilot model we can test and run out within three months, at the latest."

How would you go about designing such a "control panel"? Can it be done at all? Or is it something that sounds good and does not work in practice. What about the CEO's idea that it be the same for the whole senior management group. Is it sound?

MANAGERIAL
ORGANIZATION

PART SEVEN

Banco Mercantil
and Its Structure

Banco Mercantil is not a giant of world banking. But with assets equivalent to $8 billion it is the banking giant of one of the major Latin-American countries. Its fifty branches in the country's capital city reach almost every neighborhood. And the Banco Mercantil branch office on the main square is the most imposing building in most provincial towns and cities.

Until the late 1950s these 350 branches outside the capital city served primarily as providers of deposits to the capital. They had little lending business of their own. Ninety percent of the lending business was in the capital. In the capital too was practically all the corporate business, that is, the business with large companies. There, too, was all international business—mainly borrowing money abroad in such major centers of international finance as New York, London, or Zurich to lend to the bank's corporate customers—and investment activities including a rapidly growing business in managing pension funds of large domestic companies. Only the mortgage business—legally organized in a separate bank but operated as a division of Banco Mercantil—did substantial business in the provinces. Even that only amounted to some 20 percent of the total because most population growth was in the capital.

This began to change in the early 1960s. The capital city continued to grow, but since it was badly overcrowded, more and more of the growth occurred in what had formerly been sleepy provincial towns. The mortgage business felt this first. From 1958 on, it grew much faster outside the capital than in the capital district. Then companies began to build factories in or near provincial cities to tap their labor supply and to be closer to markets. Finally, in the mid-sixties, commercial lending began to grow rapidly in the major provincial cities as small businesses, trucking companies, shopping centers and local government offices grew up to serve the expanding population in the provincial towns, many of which were rapidly becoming fair-sized cities.

The organization of Banco Mercantil reflected the country's traditional economic structure. There was a big capital-city division, headed by the bank's president and chief executive officer himself. All 350 branches outside of the capital reported through regional headquarters to the one executive vice-president in charge of the "Zona Interior." He in turn reported to the president. Then there had been formed a corporate banking division, first within the capital-city division, then separate. This too was headed by an executive vice-president who also reported to the president. International Banking, Mortgage Banking and Fiduciary Banking (investment management, especially of pension-funds) also had evolved into separate divisions, headquartered in the main office in the capital and headed by executive vice-presidents reporting to the president. In 1960 this structure worked; by 1970 the bank had clearly outgrown it.

When a new president took over in 1974 he ordered a business plan—the first the bank had ever had. To everybody's surprise it showed that except for international banking, most future growth of the bank would take place outside of the capital city. By 1980 or 1985, the plan predicted, the share of the capital-city division in the bank's loans would be down to 30 percent from 65 percent in 1970. Corporate division loans would grow to 30 percent of total loans, of which fully one third would be to large customers head-quartered outside the capital. The "Zona Interior" branches would have 40 percent of the loans and well over 50 percent of the deposits. Most of the new business centered in seven large provincial cities, each by 1970 already with a population of well over one million people.

How should the bank be organized for this change in its markets? The new president appointed an organization task force with himself chairman. After a year of study it came up with a plan for decentralization. It provided for the setting up of eight regional "banks." One of these, the largest, would be the Banco Mercantil in the capital city—in effect the existing capital-city division. It would, as before, be headed by the bank's president. The other seven regional banks, each located in one of the provincial centers that had emerged as "key cities" in the country, would have full profit and loss responsibility and would be headed by a regional "president" who would also be an executive vice-president of the bank, and who would be in full charge of all the branches in a region in addition to being the head of the main office in his provincial capital. These seven, in turn, would report to a senior executive vice-president in the capital city who would report to the bank's president. There would be vice-presidents for corporate banking, fiduciary banking, international banking and mortgage banking, each headquartered in the capital city and reporting to the president. There would be an executive vice-president for bank operations—also in the capital city and reporting to the president. An executive committee of eight people composed of the president, the senior executive vice-president in charge of the regions, the executive VPs of corporate, fiduciary, international and mortgage banking, the operating man and the bank's lawyer would be served by a small group of staff assistants: an economist, a business-development group, a planning group and a personnel adviser.

When the plan was presented to the bank's senior executives, there was a storm of protest from the regions. They pointed out first that the plan violated the principles of genuine decentralization.

The regional executive VPs were to have full business responsibility. Yet for rapidly growing parts of their business, corporate banking, fiduciary banking, and mortgage banking, they would have no direct responsibility. These activities were going to be done by headquarters divisions. The same applied to operations—that is, to the 70 percent of the bank's costs which are people. They further objected to their subordinate status as being both wrong in terms of organization and contrary to the bank's strategy. "We expect the bank to grow the most in the regions outside of the capital city; yet the regions will still be treated as they were under the old 'Zona Interior' system and report to a capital-city executive VP rather than directly to the chief executive officer," the regional men pointed out. Finally, they strongly objected to perpetuating the tradition under which the president ran the capital-city division. "This means," they said, "that the president will have no time for us, will give us no attention, and will, inevitably, channel resources and good people to the capital city when the growth opportunities and needs are outside."

The president had to concede that the critics had a case. He therefore asked them to come up with a counter-proposal, which they did within a few weeks. Their plan provided for a president with no duties except being the bank's chief public spokesman, and its chief liaison man with the country's government, with international financial institutions such as the World Bank, and with the labor unions. In addition, he would be available as trouble shooter in dealing with the top managements of big corporate clients. But all *operating* work would be lodged in the heads of the regional banks—one for the capital city and one for each of the seven regions. They, with the head of the international division and under the chairmanship of the president would constitute the executive committee. This would meet every week for at least a whole morning (and preferably not always in the capital city but at least twice a year in each of the major regions) and would make all decisions. International would remain an operating division. Corporate would become a hybrid—in part handling relations with large corporate customers itself, in part advising the regional banks on corporate business. Operations and mortgage banking would become staff departments and confined to planning policy, auditing and training, with each region doing its own operating work and running its own mortgage business. Fiduciary, the regional men thought, should probably remain centralized for the time being. There wasn't enough fiduciary business in the regions and, anyhow, pension-fund customers (the main customers of the fiduciary division) would prefer to deal with one group of professional actuaries, economists and investment managers.

The president was appalled at this proposal—it meant, as he pointed out, that he would have almost twenty men reporting to him since there would still, of course, be a legal counsel, an economist, a business-development group and a planning group, not to mention personnel and public relations. He felt strongly that decision-making authority would be totally diffused under this plan; even minor matters would become "political" and would be decided by politicking and logrolling in an executive council in which the president could always be outvoted. He was troubled by the proposed ambiguity of the role and function of corporate banking, fiduciary banking and mortgage banking—part operating divisions, part staff advisers. He felt strongly that operations should be centralized. Above all he felt that he would not have enough to do himself and would largely become a figurehead.

It took two years and the help of a large American consulting firm to hammer out a compromise. Instead of eight regions there are five—the capital city and four regions outside. Each is headed by an executive VP who reports to the president and is a member of the executive committee. The president no longer heads the capital-city division but is a full-time chief executive officer with full power to make final decisions. International, mortgage and fiduciary banking are operating "banks"—in fact each is called a "region" headed by an executive vice-president who is a member of the executive committee and reports to the president. Corporate banking, headed by an executive VP reporting to the president and sitting on the executive committee, is a hybrid—80 percent a "bank" taking care of corporate clients directly; 20 percent an "adviser," planner, and policy maker—and above all, a trainer, for the corporate-banking business of the regional banks outside the capital city. The status of operations was left up in the air—its executive VP (also reporting to the president, also a member of the executive committee) is both "responsible to the president for setting up, initiating and running efficient banking operations and for the training and supervision of operating personnel throughout the system," *and* for "advising and counselling the regional banks in carrying out their responsibility for efficient banking operations and for training and supervising operating personnel." All other functions—economics, planning budgeting, business development, personnel, public relations, and a new marketing function that the consultants recommended, were put under a newly created senior VP of administration who attends meetings of the executive committee without being a member, and who reports to no one quite knows whom. The lawyer is, of course, still there too.

Questions for Discussion

(1) How does each of these three alternative organization structures measure up to the criteria of decentralization? Which of them comes the closest to "federal decentralization?" Could it have worked? Which of them is "simulated decentralization?" And might any of them perhaps not be "decentralization" at all but a thinly disguised functional organization?

(2) Decentralization means "decentralized operations with central control." The president's plan stressed "control," the regional heads' plan stressed "decentralized operations." The president's plan stressed the span of control—with only seven men reporting to the president. The regional heads' plan would have meant twenty men reporting to the president—clearly more than one man can supervise. But the second plan would have followed far more closely the logic of the business and the planned strategy with its expectation of rapid growth in the regional centers. How does the plan that was finally worked out satisfy these conflicting requirements of "decentralization" and "central control," of the logic of organization and the dynamics of strategy?

(3) How much sense does the new administrative VP make? Do the functions he heads belong together as building blocks of organization? What can he actually do for the highly expert professionals who report to him? Would it be better to have these functions separate and working with the executive committee as originally proposed?

Case Number 2

What Does
"Staff" Mean?

As soon as the Banco Mercantil had carried out its re-organization, the new president tackled his second priority: modernizing bank operations. By 1970 the computer had, of course, been introduced in the bank in many places, but operations were still largely a matter of local tradition. What computer use there was was uncoordinated, left to individual managers in major regions, and had largely been superimposed on existing, primarily manual systems.

The new president brought into the bank a national of the country who had gone to the U.S. for graduate study in 1952, had become interested in the computer when computers were still new, and had done pioneering work in designing computer languages for business use. Juan Perez had worked for IBM as their expert on computer use in banks and had finally headed the computer program at one of the big New York City banks. He became willing to return to his native country and to a senior position in its leading bank after his American wife died. And since the long-time executive vice-president of operations at Banco Mercantil had just reached retirement age, the bank could offer both a top-management title and a very fancy salary to lure Dr. Perez back from New York.

The first things Perez did everybody approved of. He standardized the computer equipment of the bank. Where formerly there had been eight large computers, each a different make and incompatible with the others, Perez reduced the number to five—one for each region—each much smaller and cheaper but all the same make and model and therefore capable of working together. And the plan and priorities which he submitted—the first five-year plan any one at Banco Mercantil had ever seen—was also favorably received throughout the bank.

But when he moved to carry out the plan he immediately ran into violent opposition from most of the "bankers" who ran the profit and loss centers of Banco Mercantil: the five executive vice-presidents who headed the five major geographic regions; the heads of corporate banking and of mortgage banking. Only the heads of international banking and of investment banking remained indifferent; Perez' plan did not affect their operations.

Perez had talked about "centralizing all data processing in one system" and of "running a central data switchboard." To his banking associates this sounded like a kind of central telephone network, with a computer operator who would serve the people in branches and banking offices from a central location the way a long-distance operator does in the telephone system. But Perez saw things quite differently. To him everything in a bank except obtaining money from the public and lending it out, was "data processing": check clearing, bookkeeping, deposit accounting, loan accounting, loan collections—in fact almost everything bankers traditionally call "banking." And therefore, all this work and the people doing it he claimed as being under his jurisdiction, as being managed by him, staffed by him. The people doing the work would be hired by him, supervised by him, trained by him and paid by him.

When he was accused of wanting to take over the "business" of the bank, Perez replied, "The bank's *business* is getting money and lending it and I have no intention of interfering with that. Everything else is supporting operations processing data; and that is the operating work *I* am supposed to *do*."

When told that operations had been set up as a staff department to advise the bank's managers but not to run things, he answered: "You can only advise where you can tolerate diversity; in data processing you can no more tolerate diversity than you could in the equipment and operations of a telephone system—the whole point is that it is uniform and standardized. You are quite right," he said to the bankers, "data processing is not banking work, but it isn't staff either. It is joint operational support. If you don't get what you need from me and my people, fire me. If you can get the same work done cheaper or better elsewhere, buy it there. But no matter who does it and where, it has to be done in one place, be run by one outfit and one manager. And it must be run with line authority rather than as a staff activity. All right, so it accounts for 70 percent of a bank's expenses; that's no different from a manufacturing company like General Electric in the U.S. which pays 60 to 70 percent of its gross sales for raw materials and supplies—and no one calls that 'staff.' Data records, figures are the raw materials of banking. It's my job to supply them to you—and this means I have to run the system rather than tell you how you should run it."

Questions for Discussion

(1) How does Perez's approach fit the traditional concept of "decentralization?" Does it interfere with it? Does it support it?

(2) Can the manager of a division or region still have true profit and loss respnsibility for his order division if such a "joint operational support" function controls 60 percent or more of the expenses and the bulk of the people in that division? Is it enough, in other words, to have control over, and responsibility for, the activities that produce results and revenue—getting money and lending it out—without also having control over, and responsibility for, the major cost centers? And what do you think of Dr. Perez' analogy of operational costs and the "raw materials" in a manufacturing company?

(3) Assuming that Perez wins—whether he is right or wrong—what might the bank have to do to make sure that it will have "bankers" tomorrow? Traditionally "bankers," the people who produce the money through deposits and

savings accounts and who then lend it out, have come up from "operators" such as tellers, branch managers and so on. Will that still be possible when these people are under the management and control of operations? If not, what can the bank do—either to restore channels of advancement to operating people or to build new channels?

Case Number 3

Profit Center:
Independent Business:
or Service Activity?

Dr. Perez, the Banco Mercantil's computer expert, won his argument with the "bankers" only by agreeing to separate his operations and data-processing activity from the bank itself. Banco Mercantil set it up in a wholly-owned subsidiary organized to offer data-processing and operating services commercially with the bank as first and main customer. Perez pretended to fight this, but secretly he had always believed that this was the right way to do the data-processing job. He really did believe what he had told the "bankers": that data and their processing were the "raw material" of banking and that they should therefore be organized outside, and separate from, banking. And he believed that this was just as true for many other institutions, especially for government activities. "Information is the raw material of post-industrial civilization" he had once declared in an interview that got him big headlines in the *New York Times*", way back in 1960 when the computer was still "news."

As soon as Perez had been set up in 1973 as Banco Mercantil Servicios de Computer S.A.—a wholly-owned but separate subsidiary— he began to sell integrated computer services, time-sharing, tailor-made programs and so on. No one had done this before in his

Latin American country. Some of the services Perez pioneered were then very advanced even for the U.S. As a result, Perez by 1976 had built up a large and profitable computer-services business. He did all the operational and data-processing work for his country's largest bank, Banco Mercantil, on long-term contract for a fixed fee plus a fee for every million transactions. But Banco Mercantil, while his largest customer, provided only 40 percent of his revenue. The rest came from outside customers, especially government agencies.

Banco Mercantil was happy with Perez' success until Perez was approached by one of the country's smaller banks with the request that he take it on as a customer. The bank proposed that Perez set up and run its data-processing and operating system. Banco Meridional was only one quarter the size of Banco Mercantil. But in its region—in the south of the country—it was second, and in a few important centers it was even first, beating Banco Mercantil out of the top spot. Its head—who had been a key executive of Banco Mercantil until he left in a huff when he had been passed over for the presidency in 1974—had repeatedly attacked Banco Mercantil as the "octopus" and had talked darkly of the "need to break up the banking monopoly in our country." He was not therefore regarded with much affection in the headquarters of Banco Mercantil.

Perez was careful enough to inform the president of Banco Mercantil of his new customer—but shrewd enough to do this only after he had signed the contract with him. As he had expected, there was a tremendous uproar. This "trafficking with the enemy," as some Banco Mercantil stalwarts called it, brought into the open a severe disagreement over the function of Perez' company between Perez and Banco Mercantil which owned this company. "We want you to work for us," the Banco Mercantil people said. "We expect you to give us first priority and to concentrate on our work. Only if you have time and people to spare from our work, do we want you to service others. But the others come second; we must come first. As for serving a competitor, that's out—if only because you know all our secrets and handle all our data."

"Oh, no," said Perez, "that can't work. The computer-service company is a profit center. That means we better treat it as an independent business. You are our largest customer, and you can expect and demand the best of service. But you are not entitled to anything we do not offer to all our customers, nor to a lower price. As to serving the competition, we serve anyone who is willing to pay our rather stiff fees. It's up to us to make sure that we treat every customer's information absolutely confidentially. In fact it is to *your* interest that we have outside customers. It's your best way of making sure that we do a first-rate job and that we do not over-charge you but charge you only what a competitive market pays. And by the way, if I had turned down Banco Meridional, I would only have given them ammunition in their fight against us as an 'octopus' and a 'vicious monopoly' which ought to be broken up or restrained."

It was this last point that finally convinced the Banco Mercantil people to accept Perez' contract with their competitor. But that lead to quite a bit of soul-searching regarding the proper function and role of a service activity that had been converted into a profit-making, autonomous business. Should that have been done? Should it be encouraged? And once it has been done, what are the rules?

Questions for Discussion

(1) Granting that Banco Mercantil has set up computer services as an autonomous affiliate, is Perez right in claiming that it then should be run as an independent business rather than as a service facility? And does this mean, as Perez claims, that the parent company, despite its 100 percent ownership, be treated just as another customer, neither better nor worse than outside customers?

(2) What do you think about Perez' dismissal of the claim that the line should be drawn in respect to direct competitors, especially in an area where there *is* confidential information as there is in data processing? Might such an activity from the beginning restrict itself to noncompetitors, if only to escape any suspicions of betraying secrets?

(3) Do you think the policy the Banco Mercantil people would like to adopt: preferential treatment of their bank

with sale of "surplus" services to others, could work? Is there no alternative other than either an independent business or a wholly-integrated inside activity working for the bank, only and entirely within it?

Case Number 4

The Universal Electronics Company

Universal Electronics had for many years been active in Latin America. In fact, it had done better in Latin America than in the U.S. While it never ranked higher than sixth or seventh in the U.S. electronics industry, it early became the leading manufacturer in most of the important Latin American markets. Subsidiaries in all Latin countries were managed by Universal's own managers but otherwise run and operated as local companies, employing local personnel, and manufacturing and distributing their own local brand names. By 1960, the Latin American businesses accounted for about 20 percent of the company's income even though no more than 8 percent of the company's capital was invested in them. In cheap radios and radio tubes and in transmission and telephone equipment, the Latin American businesses had shown much faster growth than those had of the U.S. parent company itself.

However, Universal had had no experience in international business except in Latin America until a chance dispute with an Italian licensee brought the company together with a young Italian lawyer, Dr. Federigo Manzoni. In 1960 Manzoni suggested that the best way to resolve the licensing dispute was to buy up the Italian licensee, a medium-sized company, badly in need of capital but with a good name and excellent technical facilities. Out of this grew Universal's present European business—five major subsidiaries, all either wholly-owned or majority-owned, all growing faster than the U.S. parent company, all more profitable—and all bought or expanded with very little money before the great growth period of the European Common Market. Manzoni himself became president of the Italian company—the fastest-growing and most profitable of the lot. Largely through his energy, his vision of the European potential, and his great negotiating skills, Universal achieved the European growth that has made it a proverbial "growth stock."

In 1964 Universal had gotten just enough license fees out of Europe to pay its European patent and license expenses. By 1977, 45 percent of Universal's income came from Europe. In Universal's ten-year plan that figure was expected to go up to 55 percent by 1985 with the absolute amount doubling within eight years.

The European business had been the "baby" of the company's president, Julian DeRoche. He had himself negotiated every major purchase in Europe. He had pushed the deals through his board of directors. He had worked, aided primarily by Manzoni, on revamping the acquired companies where necessary, on finding the first-rate people in them to whom to entrust the management, and—the most difficult job of all—on bringing together their technical and research people with those of the parent company. Beyond technical cooperation, which had become very close, and over-all financial and top-management-personnel control, the individual companies were largely left to manage themselves under their own local management group, organized according to the customs and laws of each country.

Two of the Europeans, however—Dr. Manzoni and the president of the large German affiliate—were members of the Universal board in the United States.

As a result of the European acquisitions and of U.S. space contracts, Universal grew rapidly in personnel and sales during these years. What had been a 200 million dollar company in 1960 sales, brought in close to a billion dollars ten years later. Where there had been fewer than 20,000 employees, there were, in 1977, well over 100,000—spread over five continents (as the European affiliates themselves had branches, subsidiaries or affiliates abroad).

Meanwhile DeRoche was not getting any younger. Anticipating his retirement and the need for a basic reorganization of the corporate structure, DeRoche in 1976 asked his senior staff vice-president to design an organization structure that would be adequate to the needs of an international company. Traditionally, Universal had been a functionally organized manufacturing company —with vice-presidents of research, engineering, manufacturing, marketing, finance, etc. Necessity had diluted this simple concept considerably. There was, for instance, an Executive Vice-President-Defense Production whose job cut across all conceivable organization lines. Latin America was organized in an international division which both supervised manufacturing subsidiaries and export sales and spent most of its time, it seemed to outsiders, in mysterious foreign-exchange deals no one understood. At home, the Universal Electronics Distribution Company had been set up to sell and service Universal's consumer products. But despite all these amendments, the basic functional structure of a rather small-sized manufacturing company was still Universal's fundamental organization concept.

The staff vice-president, a man trained thoroughly in organization planning in one of the big manufacturing companies before he had come to Universal in 1970 talked to a great many people in the company. He also made the circuit looking at the other major "international companies." Early in 1977 he came up with a blueprint that provided for four divisions: Defense and Space Electronics, Consumer Products, Industrial Products, and International. All activities of Universal outside the U.S. and Canada were to be lumped together in the International Division. On the president's staff and outside of this divisional structure, the plan provided for the typical "staff services"—from research to purchasing and personnel.

The staff vice-president's own candidate for the job of Division President-International was Dr. Manzoni, for whom he had great admiration. But in the course of a conversation about the progress of European unification, Manzoni pointed out that it would still be difficult to put one European national over another. And to the direct question of whether an Italian could easily be the head of a company with German, French, Dutch, British or other European affiliates, Manzoni had said bluntly that it could be done but that he would not envy the poor devil who'd have to do it. Reluctantly the staff vice-president therefore decided on another candidate, Axel Sorensen, Danish-born and a Danish educated U.S. citizen, who had headed Universal do Brasil—the largest subsidiary before the expansion in Europe. Sorensen had advanced rapidly in the U.S. organization before going out to Colombia as chief engineer. From there he went to Brazil, first as local chief engineer, then as a successful and popular local president. To strengthen Sorensen however—and also to save him travel—Manzoni was named Deputy Group President and Chief of Staff-Europe to the International Division.

When the staff vice-president showed this draft to the president, DeRoche was impressed. This was roughly what he had hoped for. "Let's, for safety's sake, check with Manzoni first," he said. "He knows the Europeans better than we do, and we ought to talk to him before taking this up with our own top people."

Accordingly the staff vice-president flew to Rome to show his outline to Manzoni. He was astounded when Manzoni—the quiet, polite, amiable Manzoni—exploded after one look at the chart. "This is both an insult and abject stupidity! I know you and like you, and I'd be willing to stay on trying to prevent your ruining your European operations if you go through with this. But I would only stay on as head of Italy. Nothing in the world would get me to take the "deputy" job and thereby compound the insanity of this approach to the organization of an 'international company.' And believe me, if the German and the Frenchman running your two companies in these two countries ever get wind of this hare-brained scheme, they will quit within the week. They don't have to work for Universal. There are plenty of jobs for first-rate people in Europe today. And they won't be treated as if they ran an Army and Navy Surplus Store in Tibet instead of a large electronics company in their own country and one that contributes as much to total earnings as any of Universal's U.S. businesses."

The outburst was so violent that the staff VP thought it better not even to try to find out what Manzoni objected to—though he was completely bewildered.

Questions for Discussion

What might it be that struck Manzoni as wrong? In what way does the staff vice-president's approach, which does not differ much from the way in which a great many U.S.

companies organize their "international" business, differ from what you or Manzoni would consider the proper organization for a truly "international business?" (One clue: Is it in line with the economic realities and expectations of the company?)

Case Number 5

The Function of the Chief Executive

Although the mandatory retirement age at this company was 65, John Neyland, the president, decided to retire at 62. He was 60 when he made this decision. He had come in as chief executive officer of the company twenty-one years earlier. During his tenure the company had grown and prospered. He enjoyed his work, but lately he had noticed a tendency to tire more rapidly than in the past. Also Neyland, a devoted churchman, felt that he could contribute a good deal to his church, and especially to the colleges affiliated with it. For the last five years, he had served on the board of advisers for higher education of his church. He had greatly enjoyed the work and had felt that he was not really doing as much as was needed—especially at a time like the present when the colleges were faced with tremendous demands for money, facilities, and faculty, let alone with serious questions regarding their educational policy.

But what convinced John Neyland to step out earlier than he had to was the fact that he felt sure of having a first-rate successor. When Neyland had joined the company, Bill Strong was a very young accountant, fresh out of college. He was, however, already considered a very able man. When Neyland needed a young analyst to help him with a difficult tax negotiation during the Vietnamese War, Strong had been put on his staff. Shortly thereafter Strong became Assistant to the President and, three years ago, vice-president in charge of administration. Neyland felt certain that Strong could easily step into his job, felt indeed that Strong was likely to do a better job than he himself had done.

Before Neyland announced his intention to the board, he thought it best to discuss it with his closest and oldest friend on the board, the man who, many years earlier, had brought him to the company and who represented the largest and most influential group of shareholders. This friend agreed with Neyland's decision to retire early. But he disagreed violently with Neyland's nomination of Strong as his successor. "You know," he said, "that I have never voted against management, and that it is against my principles to do so. But if you propose Strong as your successor, I will vote against him and will make an issue of it. There is a capable successor in the company, but it is not Strong. It is Margaret Wetherall, your vice-president of manufacturing. Strong has never in his life done any operating work. He has been a staff man all along. His only experience is in finance. Wetherall on the other hand started out as a design-engineer, has been a sales manager, and has now run manufacturing for ten years. She really knows the business. And also, Strong has never had an independent responsibility. He has always been an assistant to you rather than responsible for results himself."

Neyland protested. "But look at the jobs Strong has done. You yourself have considered them outstanding. Strong did most of the thinking behind the basic change in our direction fifteen years ago to which we owe our growth. He does all the thinking behind our financing. And he has really been the one who has developed people and made the decisions whom to put where. It was his courage that shifted Margaret Wetherall out of the sales job into manufacturing management. He is by far the best thinker we have. And you yourself have stressed often enough that he is a man of courage and integrity. Wetherall is a perfectly fine operating manager. But she has neither the imagination nor the ability to think that is needed for the top job."

"I don't think, John," his friend answered, "we will get anywhere on this by discussing people. You have made up your mind for Strong; I have made up my mind against him. But we ought not to talk people. We ought to talk about the function of the chief executive and the job to be done. It is there, I think, that we disagree. I think we agree on the qualities of the individuals. Why don't you go back and think through what, in your mind, the chief executive of this company has to do, what he is responsible for, what his function is and what his qualification ought to be. I'll do the same. I'm sure we won't agree—otherwise we would have agreed on the candidate. But at least after we have done this, we will be able to find out why we disagree. And I think you and I better agree before we bring this up with our colleagues on the board."

What do you think is John Neyland's concept of the functions of the chief executive? How does his friend see the job? By the way, do you think the friend is right in starting out with an objective idea of the function? Or do you think it would be better to begin with an outstanding candidate—or candidates—and then adapt the job to what he or she is and how he or she does the work?

Case Number 6

Research Coordination in the Pharmaceutical Industry

One of the country's, and the world's, largest pharmaceutical companies has major research laboratories in five countries: The United States; Great Britain; Ireland; France; and Japan. The laboratory in the U.S. goes back to the 1920s. The one in Great Britain grew out of the work in World War II, when the company was among the pioneers in large-scale production of penicillin. The fundamental knowledge about antibiotics was then still primarily in Great Britain so that the necessary massive scientific and technical effort had to be based there. The Irish laboratory was a by-product of the decision to take advantage of exceedingly favorable Irish tax laws when locating a major new plant—a plant meant to produce intermediates primarily for the European market. Since the techniques used in the plant were mostly new, there was a need for a substantial group of technical and scientific plant-chemists, as well as plant-engineers. This made it logical for the Irish Government to suggest that the company build a full-sclae research lab, if only to hold well-trained Irish scientists in Ireland rather than have them emigrate to the U.K., the U.S., and Canada, and logical that the company pick up the suggestion. France was chosen for a laboratory in veterinary products, an old French specialty and one in which French government and French universities gladly cooperate with industry. Also, the French scientists the company wanted for the work were rather cool to the idea of moving to the United States and positively icy about the alternative suggestion: to move to the British midlands and to exchange the climate and scenery of the Loire for the fogs of Manchester. Japan first came with a joint venture. But when the American company bought out the Japanese partner in 1968, as the Japanese business grew so fast and so successfully that the Japanese could no longer finance it, it had to take over a large, flourishing, and completely Japanese lab. At first only one man understood enough English to participate intelligently in the company's annual world-wide research conference. But that did not stop the Japanese from doing first-rate work in tropical medicine in which none of the company's other labs had much competence or strength.

However, ALL five labs complained that there wasn't any coordination between them, that there was constant duplication of effort, and, worse still, that important and promising work wasn't being done at all because each lab thought the other one was doing it, and that no one in any of the five labs really knew where to go in the other four to find help, to get advice and to talk over matters of common interest.

This was the situation when a new company-wide research vice-president took over. Or rather, Dr. Rodney VanDelden—Dutch-born, American-educated, chief biochemist in the British lab until he moved to America around 1968 to finish a research job on central-nervous system drugs the American group had botched—was really the FIRST company-wide research chief ever. His predecessor had still been Research Director in the US, the first among five equals, and expected only to "coordinate". VanDelden was expected to MANAGE, and had, as visible sign of his new authority, control of the budgets of all research labs whereas formerly each country had set and managed the research budget for its own research efforts.

What alternatives does VanDelden have? What problems can he anticipate? What patterns of coordination and organization are available to him? And how could he test each of them to see which might be applicable in this multi-national, multi-lingual, multi-disciplinary, and multi-cultural setting?

Case Number 7

The Aftermath
of Tyranny

The Rasumofsky Company, makers of "59" brand insecticides and industrial chemicals, had been run for many years by one man: Ferdinand Bullock, who was largely responsible for its steady growth during the last seventeen years. Bullock was actually the boss in all but title even before he was made Executive Vice President in 1959. Since then, however, he had controlled everything in the company and made every important decision.

The President had confined himself to handling a few old customers—who a quarter century earlier had accounted for the bulk of the company's sales, and whose loyalty and, on one occasion, financial help had pulled the company through the great depression. By now, however, these customers accounted only for ten percent or less of the company's business—a result of the expansion since Bullock had become the dominant force in the company. The President, in other words, was not much more than an assistant sales manager except in title.

The other officers of the company were all Bullock's office boys and treated by him as such. The only one showing signs of independence was Stanley Greenback, the Assistant Controller, who had come in from the company's public accounting firm four years earlier to handle tax matters; but he was still very young and had had no experience except in auditing and taxes.

The Chairman of the Board—the last representative of the Rasumofsky family that had started the company and had originally owned it entirely—had been worrying about the situation for quite some time. But he consoled himself with the thought that there was plenty of time—after all, Bullock was a young man, barely 55, and had at least another ten years to go. And there was no doubt but that the company prospered under his reign. Also, secretly, the Chairman had little stomach for a fight with Bullock and was even afraid that in such a fight the other major stockholders, including various Rasumofsky widows, nieces and grand-daughters, would side with Bullock against him. The bulk of the shares, by the way, was owned by small share-holders outside. It had been fairly widely distributed when the company became publicly owned in 1928; and Bullock controlled the proxy machine.

THEN SUDDENLY, IN EARLY 1977, BULLOCK DIED OF A HEART ATTACK. On paper that should have made little difference; in fact the Organization Chart looked prettier without him and with the functional VP's reporting directly to the President. But actually the company was without a head.

At the same time Bullock's death released an emotional storm that had long been suppressed by his heavy hand. It became clear, even to the not too observant President and Chairman, that Bullock had governed through fear and intimidation, that he had systematically driven out or broken men of independence and spirit and had replaced them with yes-men, and that even his own creatures in the vice-presidential seats would not accept another "one-man regime." But, alas, it became also clear that not one of the VPs was able to stand on his own feet and to make his own decisions; they had all been too dependent on the strong man too long.

1. What do you think the company can do?

2. Any general conclusions and observations on management theory and management practice?

STRATEGY
AND STRUCTURE

PART EIGHT

What is the Contribution
of Bigness?

Founded in the 1890s, the Miller Tool Company had been growing
unspectacularly for seventy years when a new president took over
around 1960. During the Depression, the company had almost been
forced into receivership. But during and since World War II, it had
become a leader in the design and manufacturing of metal-working
machinery. The new president, McFettridge, however, felt,
strongly that the prosperity of the company would be short-lived
unless it did two things. First, branch out of the traditional
mechanical machine tools into the new electronic tools which
McFettridge saw clearly coming in the course of automation. However, the company had no knowledge in the field of electronics at
all. Secondly, McFettridge argued that the company had to

counter-balance its exclusive dependence on the heavy industries by a stake in industries that were less vulnerable to economic fluctuations.

The company had sometime during the 1920s obtained a listing on the New York Stock Exchange. Hence, McFettridge could offer to the owners of small companies an exchange of their unlisted shares against listed shares with their tax advantages and greater liquidity. Armed with this, the considerable cash in the company's treasury and its reputation, McFettridge stepped out systematically to acquire new businesses.

First, McFettridge acquired five electronic companies, all small and all highly specialized. To "diversify" the company's economic risk, he then added six companies in various service businesses, among them a trucking company, a building maintenance business, a construction company specializing in schools, highways and other public works, a small chain of dry cleaning stores, etc. He also bought seven small businesses that could not easily be classified, businesses that appeared to him to be sound growth investments and available at a reasonable price. The largest of them was a baking company with a good position in the Southeast, which McFettridge considered a growth region.

McFettridge died suddenly in 1969, at the time when the company he had built had acquired a reputation as an aggressive growth company and had become a favorite investment for some of the more adventurous of the investment and pension funds. Since he was still quite a young man, nobody had thought of replacing him; and there was no one in the company who could take over.

The directors brought in an experienced industrial manager, Henry Augener, who, a few years before had left the vice-presidency of one of the big appliance companies to become a partner in a management consulting firm. Augener, who came in as President, brought along with him Eugene De Witt, a younger man with a sound financial background.

The two men spent several months examining the company. What they found appalled them. Augener had been warned by some of his friends before he took the job that there was trouble ahead and that things were by no means as rosy as they looked in the write-ups of the financial analysts. But reality was much worse than anything anybody on the outside expected.

In the first place, none of the new acquisitions really had much of a business. The old Miller Tool Company with its seventy million dollars of sales contributed about a quarter of the company's sales and a considerably larger share of the company's profits. The largest of the additional businesses had only about fifteen million dollars in sales—the baking company; and the smallest had barely two million. Miller Tool, in other words, consisted of a large number of small businesses.

At the same time, these businesses had not been integrated with one another but had remained completely separate—and it was hard to see how they could be integrated. None of the electronics businesses had contributed anything to the machine tool business. On the contrary, each of them was developing along its own lines. One of them was exclusively engaged in research work for the armed forces. Another one made component parts for the television industry in which it had to compete against very large and efficient manufacturers turning out the same component parts by the million. The technological changes which McFettridge had anticipated eight years earlier in respect to the machine tool business were slowly coming in; but Miller still had the same tools it had had during World War II. And it was clear that any change in the business cycle would result in a sharp deterioration for Miller with its obsolescent product line. At the same time, many of the good people at Miller had been sucked into the new businesses which were in dire need of first-rate engineers and designers, so that Miller's design staff had become denuded of men and of ideas.

Things were in a similar state in the service businesses.

Even after six months of hard study, Augener and De Witt did not really quite know what the company had in its miscellaneous businesses, and where those were headed for. But while it was very clear that things were not in good shape, it was very difficult to say what could or should be done.

It was, for instance, quite clear that the company should get out of some of its businesses. But which ones should be divested? The ones with the least growth potential were also the businesses that contributed the most cash to the parent company—and cash was badly needed. At the same time the companies with the best long-range potential for growth and profit were also those that needed the most cash, that indeed needed much more cash than the company could generate or obtain, and that also were particularly risky or made particularly high demands on technological leadership.

But the most pressing area was that of top management. It was clear to Augener and De Witt that the company needed a top management. McFettridge had run the show himself. He had brought in a large number of "bright young boys" whom he used as his messengers. But he himself, huddling with his "bright young boys", had made all the decisions. Augener and De Witt realized that there had to be a management at the top.

Equally important there had to be management of the businesses. McFettridge had been able to get a number of businesses at very reasonable terms because he offered a way out to elderly owner-managers who had reached retirement age. These men themselves usually ran a very thin management; and when they pulled out there was no one there. Then McFettridge had "replaced" them by taking over the management of the different businesses himself.

Augener and De Witt realized clearly that there had to be a management responsible for the performance of a business. But first: what was a business in their situation? Secondly, where would a management come from? Good professional managers, they realized, would hardly be interested in taking over such very small businesses. Entrepreneurs on the other hand, would much prefer to build their own business and to develop an ownership stake.

But the central question to which they returned again and again was that of corporate top management, its function, its structure, and its responsibility.

The two men spent several months in fruitless discussions and analysis without being able to reach any decision where and how to begin the difficult job. One day De Witt said: "Look here, we are never going to get anywhere trying to talk about any one of the individual businesses. We have to find a general approach. And we have to start out from the few things we can take as proven, we can assume are so."

"We know that this is a company with three hundred million dollars sales or so, that engaged in a lot of highly technical businesses in very competitive fields. We know, therefore, that it has to have the management of a big company, with its formal structure, with its highly paid specialists, and so on. We know that this management must contribute something to justify its very high cost. This we know—everything else we are merely guessing at. So let's start out with the fact that this is a big company which requires a big-company management. What is the contribution which bigness and the management appropriate to it makes to a business? What is the justification for the expense? And which of our businesses are actually or potentially businesses that can justify, if not demand, big-business management? It seems to me that this is our first question. Those businesses which are not and will not be the kind of businesses suitable for big-business management, are definitely not for us. We ought to get rid of them regardless of the cash they produce or the growth opportunities they have, if only because they will never realize the growth opportunities under this big-company management. The others we will have to find a way to manage."

Augener thought a while and answered: "You know Gene, this sounds plausible, but there are two things that bother me, two things I don't think I understand. First, I'm not quite convinced that there are lines of business that are 'small-business' or 'big-business.' I always thought that you develop the management that fits the size you deal with—and here you talk about businesses that are suitable for small-business management or for big-business management. What exactly do you mean? How do the two differ?"

"And secondly, I am bothered by an implication in your approach: that a management should be able to manage, regardless of the industry or the line of business, only if certain management approaches and management methods, namely those applicable to big-business, are valid. Is there no limit to the number of businesses or their diversity which one management can organize and manage?"

What do you think of these two questions? And how would you answer them?

Case Number 2

General Motors and the Small Imported Car

Around 1936, G.M. management came to the conclusion that G.M. could not take a larger market share of the American automobile market than it then had—around 50 to 55 per cent—without running into severe anti-trust problems. So G.M.'s top management decided to keep its market share and to optimize the return from it. This meant, in effect, concentration on the biggest and most profitable segments of the market and maximum (or at least optimum) return—but also prices high enough to hold an umbrella over the competitors (then primarily Chrysler as Ford was still ten years away from being turned around) rather than taking advantage of G.M.'s productivities—known to be substantially higher than those of any one else—and enlarge G.M.'s market share.

The policy worked for 35 years or so. When the compacts came in, G.M. let American Motors develop the market. Then it moved in; developed its own compacts and soon had the same 50 to 55 per cent share of that market segment, with far higher profitability per car than any of the competitors. But when the foreign small imported cars—Volkswagen, above all—began to appear in the U.S. in the mid-1950s and early 1960s G.M. faced a dilemma. It could then, probably quite easily, have nipped that competition in the bud by developing its own sub-compacts; indeed in Germany it did exactly that and soon re-established its position vis-a-vis VW and Fiat. But that would have either meant to exceed the 50 per cent market share and thus invite anti-trust attention, or to give up market share in higher priced and far more profitable cars. At that time, G.M. was very much under the anti-trust gun. Dupont had just been ordered to divest itself of its holdings of G.M. shares; there were anti-trust suits regarding G.M.'s truck and bus business, its earth moving business, and its locomotive business. At the same time the profit margins on the small imported cars were ludicrously low—Volkswagen probably never made a profit on its American sales since the only saving was in steel and shipping costs while labor costs and the costs of molds and dies are pretty much the same regardless of weight and size (and engine costs are probably higher on smaller engines); and steel and shipping costs together are hardly more than 12 per cent of the costs of a car, while the price of the imported sub-compact was around 30 per cent below that of the compacts and 50 per cent or more below that of the "standard" cars which then still had almost half of the U.S. automobile market. So G.M. decided not to bother with the sub-compacts and to concentrate where its strengths and its profits were—and until 1974 or 1975 (when all automobile manufacturers fared badly, and the makers of small cars such as VW or Fiat or the Japanese worst of all) the decision worked fine for G.M. It steadily increased sales and profits while holding its 50 to 55 per cent share of the total market for U.S.-made cars. But in the meantime, of course, the market share of the imports grew steadily—first the Germans then the Japanese—until in 1975 it rose to be close to a quarter of the total American market. And only then did G.M. decide to go into the small-car business—perhaps too late.

A policy that worked well for almost forty years can hardly be called a failure. Yet there are some people in G.M. who argue that the 1935 decision was a mistake and could have been seen as a mistake even then. Indeed, ten years later, when G.M. reconverted from World War II production back to automotive work for the civilian market, several high executives in G.M. (though no one of the top management group) argued that the 1935 decision had been wrong. They did not question that G.M. could not take more than 50 per cent or so of the U.S. market; but they questioned whether the conclusion to hold G.M.'s market share to that figure and thereby hold an umbrella over competition was the right, let alone the only, decision G.M. could make.

Can you tackle this as a problem in *decision-making principles*. Never mind the automobile market which, we assume, G.M. knows inside out while we know nothing about it.

Case Number 3

Electromechanical Industries and Its European Affiliates

Electromechanical Industries is not one of the world's giants. But it is one of the very oldest of multinational companies. Its origins go back to the 1870s and to patents on automatic railroad signalling devices taken out by a young American. He aggressively marketed his devices throughout the world, mostly by going into partnership with a local mechanic or small manufacturer who both assembled the devices and sold them on the local market. By 1900, in fact, the Russian subsidiary or affiliate was actually larger than the US parent company and had a monopoly on supplying the Russian railroads. But the affiliates equally established themselves as the preferred suppliers of automatic signalling devices for railroads in Germany, France, Austria, Italy, Japan—everywhere but in Great Britain. Because these local companies were usually partnerships with a national of the country, they had their own names and were not identified with the American parent. The French company, for instance, was (and is) *"Ateliers de Valence"* after the small town at the gateway to the Province where the original shop was situated; the German company was (and is) *"Ludwig Pfannenkuchen GmbH"* after the Rhineland mechanic who was the original German partner; and it is still located in the city of Aachen in the extreme West of Germany, only a few miles from the Belgian border, where Mr. Pfannenkuchen came from.

Slowly the company expanded its product line—though it always stayed in the field of automatic or semi-automatic controls. It developed early in this century, the first fully automatic safety controls for machinery, such as the bar that prevents the drop hammer from falling down as long as a hand or other object is above the impact surface. It developed the automatic controls for aircraft wings and ailerons which are standard on all American-made planes. In 1914 it got into automatic fire controls and greatly expanded this area during World War II, for guns, tanks, aircraft and so on. Gradually the company began to buy up the shares its original partners had held in its various overseas affiliates, largely because the partner's heirs rarely had any interest in the business. By 1970 it held all, or practically all, of the capital of all its European affiliates. Still, it kept the original names. No one tried to conceal the American ownership; but to the Europeans, including probably most of the people who worked for them, these companies were German, French, Italian, Swedish or Spanish companies—no small asset, considering that most of their business was with the government.

But time showed up the problem in this loose organization, in which every chief executive officer reported directly to company headquarters in Pennsylvania—and that only rarely—while no one else in his company (except once in a while the treasurer) even knew where Pennsylvania was. By 1970, the company was becoming a victim of European integration, especially of attempts to centralize and coordinate buying for the government-owned railroad systems in the Common Market and of defense coordination in NATO. Also with the collapse of the European aircraft industry, both in respect to civilian transports and to military planes, and the almost complete switch to American-designed planes, there was need for coordination of parts-supply and, perhaps even more, of repair and maintenance services throughout Europe and across national boundaries. Above all, a good many decisions affecting the company and its products, on standardization especially of safety equipment, on railroad standardization and maintenance, and on aircraft buying and maintenance, were now being made, or at least influenced by European agencies, mostly located in Brussels or nearby.

The Europeans actually forced the hand of Electromechanical's top management. They began to complain that they lacked coordination and that it took just too long to go through Pennsylvania every time. They pointed out that with business becoming increasingly European, they found themselves again and again competing against one another and throwing the sale to a competitor by knocking each other. They pointed out that while most of the European companies were fairly small businesses by themselves, the total European business was a big, indeed a very big, business at least by European standards, with some 450 million dollars in sales and some 18,000 or 20,000 employees and that they needed services: computer services; sophisticated financial controls and foreign-exchange management; legal services; labor relation services; management-development; technical services and so on, which no one affiliate, even the biggest of them (i.e. either the German or the French company which ran neck to neck) could afford. Pennsylvania wasn't a bit happy about this. Indeed it suspected, and probably with good reason, that the Europeans were pulling a fast one and were using "European integration" as a pretext to move control from the US into their hands, or at least to interpose a layer of control which they would dominate, between themselves and US headquarters. Pennsylvania had, however, to admit that the traditional pattern in which a dozen separate European companies reported separately to corporate headquarters, no longer functioned. So, in the spring of 1973, Electromechanical Industries organized a European headquarters in Brussels and put in a "Group President-Europe".

Who would fill this spot seemed to decide itself, or so Pennsylvania thought. Both the French and the Italian top man who had the seniority, declined the honor, on grounds of age, but also because neither had the slightest desire to leave his country and move to Brussels. That really left only Dr. Otto Kruse, the 52-year old head of the German company, and, so Pennsylvania thought (and most Europeans agreed), the ablest and most accomplished man in the group. In addition, Kruse lived in Aachen, only two or three hours drive away from Brussels. While he gave up the presidency of the German company, he could keep his residence in Aachen and could continue as a professor at the Aachen Technical University, driving to Brussels on Tuesday evening and returning to Aachen three days later for the weekend and two days of teaching. But, to make doubly sure that the European companies did not feel that they were being subordinated to the German company, Pennsylvania laid down that: (1) every head of every European company still had unrestricted access to company top management in the US; and (b) that the role of the new Group President was to be primarily coordinating and that he had direct line responsibility only for "European" business like NATO.

The first indication that things weren't going well came only six months later when Electromechanical's French subsidiary lost the renewal of a contract for signalling equipment with the French Navy, a contract it and its predecessors had had since the eighteen-nineties. Electromechanical's President tried to get an explanation from the president of the French company, but he only got excuses. So he went to Paris himself and to the French banker who had financed the French affiliate company for almost a century. "French law," the French banker told him a few days later, "allows the French Navy to prefer a French company to a foreign one; an American company—and of course, the navy knows who owns Ateliers de Valence—that's not too bad. But a German one, for the French Navy? It's a little bit too early for that". And when the American sputtered in protest, his banker friend said: "Why, in the name of all that's holy, didn't you put an American into Brussels as any sensible European would have told you to do?"

What would you do if you were in the shoes of the American president? What could you do?

Case Number 4

VOLKSWAGEN'S BEETLE—
in Germany the US and Brazil

In the early 1970s, it became painfully obvious that Volkswagen's "beetle" was dying in Europe. It had enjoyed an even longer run than Henry Ford's "Model T", just about twenty years of leadership. But it was rapidly becoming totally obsolete in Europe, its original and always its main market—still about 40 per cent of "beetle" sales in 1971 or so. In the US, however, the "beetle" was still doing quite well. While no longer growing in sales, it held its own, though with a steadily diminishing lead over its competitors among foreign cars, especially the Japanese which, around 1971, were beginning their US sales push in earnest. And in Brazil, by 1971 already as large as a "beetle" market as in the US, the "beetle" was still in its lusty infancy and was expected to have ahead of itself another ten years of very fast growth before becoming obsolescent.

For the European market, VW management had prepared some likely successors to the "beetle". But it faced a problem. It needed manufacturing space for these new models—and it had no capital to build them and had never earned enough to be attractive to investors. The logical thing to do was to use space taken up by the "beetle". But how then could the still large and still healthy American "beetle" market be supplied? All of the "beetles" sold in the US were made and assembled in Germany.

There was also a problem in Brazil. Demand was growing nicely, about 10 per cent a year or so. But the only economical plant to be built in Campinas near Sao Paulo where Volkswagen do Brazil has its headquarters, or, for that matter, anywhere else in Brazil— would have been a plant about four to five times as large as the increased demand expected within the next few years, say until 1980. Volkswagen-Germany could not supply such a sum—it needed all the capital it could get for Germany. And no Brazilian investor would possibly be willing to lock up his money for six or seven years before seeing adequate profits to get it back—especially as Volkswagen do Brazil, like the German parent company, never had produced much by way of profit.

There were also foreign-exchange problems in Brazil. There was, as yet, not sufficient production of high-quality foundry iron in Brazil to step up engine production. The brakes and steering wheels, which require high-quality plastics, offered similar problems. Yet, the Brazilian authorities, conscious of a precarious foreign-exchange situation, would not have approved of importing these high-cost items but would have demanded that Volkswagen do Brazil make the enormous investment in producing them first—before having a market for the cars into which the engines, the brakes and the steering wheels were to go. In Germany, however, the company, with declining sales of the "beetle" had very large facilities for making these items, facilities that could not easily be converted into making parts for the successors to the "beetle", all of which were radically different cars (e.g. water-cooled rather than air-cooled, and with an engine mounted in front), thus requiring different engines, different brakes and a different steering train.

In this situation, a newly appointed chief executive officer of Volkswagen—the man who had built Volkswagen do Brazil in the first place—worked out a perfect strategy. Volkswagen-Germany would phase out the "beetle" and thus gain the manufacturing space it needed for the "beetle's" successor. Volkswagen do Brazil would build the large economical plant—but for sheet-metal work and assembly only and not for engines or brakes or steering train. The cars made in Brazil in excess of what the Brazilian market could take, would, during the first few years, be sold to the US and would take over supplying the US market from the German company. They would, however, first be shipped to Emden, the German North Sea port where VW has assembled cars for the US market for a long time, fitted there with engines, brakes and steering train and then sent on to the US—at only a trifling extra cost in shipping. In the meantime, while the Brazilian market was growing to absorb all Brazil's capacity and to justify building engine plants, brake plants and steering-train plants in Brazil, VW would be able to introduce its new models into the US by exporting from Germany until it knew which ones sold so that it then could build an assembly plant in America. Financially this would mean that little or no new money would be needed for German plants while the money for the Brazilian expansion could be raised against anticipated orders from America, that is through ordinary and cheap commercial loans. The Brazilians were enthusiastic when they heard about the plan. But in both Germany and the US it ran immediately into heavy weather. The first to object were the German trade unions. "Shifting beetle production to Brazil and out of Germany exports German jobs. We won't allow it", they said. "And as to building a plant in the US, even if it's only an assembly plant, forget it". They agreed that labor costs in Germany had become so high that German-made VW's can be sold in the US only at a loss—and even so were priced too high. But the remedy for this, they argued, like unions everywhere, is for the Americans to pay their underpaid workers more, not for poor German workers to lose their jobs to overpaid American workers. And the German government, the central government and various state governments—which hold the majority of VW stock—fully agreed.

But the Americans also screamed. "We can sell a German-made car here if it's priced properly, they said. We might be able to sell an American-made VW here, although a lot of the mystique will be gone. But who'd buy a car 'made in Brazil'? We'd be the laughing-stock of the market. We have too much at stake to misuse the American market as a dumping ground for surplus production the Brazilians cannot sell in their own territory. And while the American unions accept an import from Germany—grudgingly—because, after all, Germany is one of America's very best customers, and while, for the same reason, they will put up with any other European and even a Japanese car—large automobile imports from Brazil with its notoriously low wage rates (never mind that labor costs are high because productivity is so low—have you ever seen a union leader who can understand that, or a politician?) will provoke a reaction that may destroy the acceptance of the VW—any model, including your future German ones—we have worked so hard to build up."

The new chief executive officer's plan was shelved. Indeed he was fired—largely because his proposal to build an assembly plant in the US had alienated the labor unions and with them the politicians. As a result: Volkswagen in Germany fell five years behind in its new models—and may never recover from the delay. In the US the new models could not be introduced,there wasn't enough production. But the "beetle" has become so expensive—still being made in, and shipped from, Germany· with a mark-up rate 20 per cent higher against the dollar than a few years ago—that it is slipping fast and has lost its first-place position among imports. Yet its costs are so high, in US dollars especially, that the company is probably losing on every car it ships to the US—and it no longer has income from European car sales to offset these losses. And Volkswagen do Brazil, instead of being able to exploit its leadership in the world's most rapidly growing automobile market, is just inching forward—and there is a rumor that it will have to sell out a major share in the company either to a Brazilian financial group or, more probably, to a Japanese-American group (one candidate is Isuzu Motors, now 27½ per cent owned by GM which would actually act for GM. Volkswagen do Brazil would then be merged with the small GM subsidiary already operating in Brazil—and this probably would give GM control).

Could the VW chief executive officer of a few years ago, have foreseen these reactions? Could—or should—he have acted differently? Did he have any real alternatives? And what does this edifying story tell you about the realities of world economy and world market?